BEYOND DISTANCE TEACHING TOWARDS OPEN LEARNING

EDITED BY VIVIEN E. HODGSON,
SARAH J. MANN AND ROBIN S. SNELL

The Society for Research into Higher Education
& Open University Press

Open University Press
Open University Education Enterprises Limited
12 Cofferidge Close
Stony Stratford
Milton Keynes MK11 1BY, England

and

242 Cherry Street
Philadelphia, PA 19106, USA

First published 1987

British Library Cataloguing in Publication Data

Beyond distance teaching, towards open learning.
  1. Distance education
  I. Hodgson, Vivien E. II. Mann, Sarah J.
  III. Snell, Robin IV. Society for
Research into Higher Education
  371.3   LC5800

ISBN 0-335-15603-7

Library of Congress Cataloguing in Publication Data

Beyond distance teaching towards open learning.
  Bibliography: p.
  Includes index.
  1. Distance education. I. Hodgson, Vivien E.
  II. Mann, Sarah J. III. Snell, Robin. IV. Society
for Research into Higher Education.
  LC5800.B49 1987   378'.03   87-5781

ISBN 0-335-15603-7

Typeset by Burns and Smith, Derby
Printed in Great Britain

CONTENTS

FOREWORD

As we approach the end of the twentieth century we are entering a strange new world. The depth of the transformation has been well documented by J.W. Botkin et al. in *No Limits to Learning,* E. Faure et al. in *Learning to Be,* J. Naisbitt in *Megatrends,* D. Schon in *Beyond the Stable State,* A. Toffler in *Learning for Tomorrow* and in *The Third Wave,* and others. And all agree that to prepare our people to survive, much less flourish, in this new world we need a new kind of education.

Botkin and his associates propose that we need to replace our current 'maintenance' education, which gives people the knowledge and skills necessary to function in the world as it is now, with 'innovative' or 'adaptive' education, which enables people to engage in continuous change. Faure and his associates propose that our whole educational enterprise needs to be reorganized around the concept of lifelong learning. Naisbitt emphasizes the need to gear all of our societal institutions to an information society. Schon proposes that both our governance and educational systems must be geared to functioning in an unstable state. Toffler points to the need to develop a new species of humanity (a third wave) that is highly proficient in taking autonomous responsibility, especially for their own learning. It seems to me that this is the direction in which the present book on open learning is also moving.

As I see it, several fundamental (as contrasted to shallow) forces are at work shaping the new world. Perhaps the most impactful force is the accelerating pace of change. This is a brand new phenomenon in our civilization. As Schon points out, we have experienced change during the last two centuries and have learned to adapt to it. The Industrial Revolution produced change, but it was a relatively stable and gradual change. For the last several decades the *pace* of change has been increasing, with the knowledge explosion and the technological revolution. The half-life of knowledge and required skills, attitudes and values is shrinking at a faster and faster pace. The rate of human obsolescence is growing exponentially, and is especially evident in the health care and high-tech fields. But it is evident in the field of management, too. The people who were effective in managing the relatively stable organizations of a few decades ago are ineffective in managing the highly volatile organizations of the present and what promise to be even more volatile organizations in the future. We must provide mechanisms to enable managers to continue to acquire new knowledge and develop new skills, attitudes and values day in and day out at a time, place, and pace that is convenient to them in their busy lives. It is just such mechanisms that this book addresses.

A second force, which is probably just a special facet of the first, is the rapid development of electronic media for delivering educational services. I am convinced that most educational services will be delivered electronically within a couple of decades. But we are just beginning to discover how to use such media for educational purposes. We are discovering that there are two keys to their effective use for learning. One key is *interaction.* Learning is an interactive process — the learner interacting with his or her environment. And there are two ways of building interaction into a media programme. The first is by interaction between the learner and the programme. In Chapter 7, Rhodes distinguishes between linear programming, which produces 'reactive' interaction, and branching programming, which provides for 'proactive' and 'coactive' interaction, in which the learner is much more self-directing. The second way is by interaction among two or more learners and between them and the programme. Particularly in distance learning is provision for interaction among learners crucial.

A second key to the effective use of media for learning is what the media specialists call *high-tech/high touch,* by which they mean building a human touch into the media programme. The 'proactive' and 'coactive' processes described in Chapter 7 give the learners a sense of interacting with a human being, not just a machine. Some computer programmes I use provide a biographical sketch of the person who wrote the programme and ask my name; and subsequent responses are to me by name from the programmer by name. Other ways of retaining a human touch in media programmes are described in this book (Chapters 2 and 5).

A third fundamental force that affects the world of education is the explosion of knowledge in the last couple of decades about learning, especially adult learning. Until the mid-fifties educational psychologists focused their research on teaching, particularly the teaching of children and youth. As a result, our entire educational system was organized around the concepts of pedagogy (the art and science of teaching children). In the mid-fifties research began to be done on adult learning and it was discovered that adults possessed certain unique characteristics as learners that were violated by the pedagogical model. An alternative, andragogical (the art and science of helping adults learn) model evolved. It identified several characteristics of adults that must be taken into account for their effective learning.

First, adults have a deep psychological need to be self-directing. In fact, the psychological definition of 'adult' is 'one who has achieved the self-concept of being responsible for his or her own life.' When adults experience others imposing their decisions on them, they resist carrying out those decisions. We run into a special problem with this phenomenon in anything labelled 'education'. People have been so deeply conditioned by their previous educational experience to perceive education as 'being taught' that they are initially uncomfortable about being asked to take responsibility for their own learning. Accordingly, a good deal of attention has been given recently in adult education to developing strategies that will help adults make the transition from dependent to self-directing learners.

Secondly, adults come into any educational activity with a broad variety of life experiences. Learning programmes for adults must therefore make provision for the individualization of learning plans and for learners to make use of each other's resources (for some kinds of learning, the resources of peers are the richest resources).

Thirdly, adults become ready to learn when they experience the need to know or be able to do something in order to be more effective. Programmes for adults are therefore based upon an analysis of their life tasks or problems.

Fourthly, adults enter into an educational activity with a life-centred, task centred or problem-centred orientation to learning, not a subject-centred one. Accordingly, learning experiences for adults are organized around life situations, not subject-matter units.

Fifthly, adults are motivated more potently by intrinsic motivators, such as increased self-esteem, more challenging responsibilities or more creative self-expression, and less by extrinsic motivators such as punishments or rewards.

The open learning approaches described and discussed in this book seem to me to be more congruent with these characteristics of adult learners than the traditional management development approaches they are rapidly replacing.

The most significant premise of the book, it seems to me, is that as we move into the strange new world of the future we must provide an educational enterprise that makes learning resources accessible to people at their convenience in terms of time, place and pace through their life span. That is what distance teaching and open learning are all about.

I am grateful to the editors for providing this resource for helping us to move into the twenty-first century.

Malcolm S. Knowles
Professor Emeritus
North Carolina State University
Raleigh, North Carolina
June 1986

INTRODUCTION AND ACKNOWLEDGEMENTS

This book is made up of papers provoked by a conference at the University of Lancaster in September 1985 on the issues in theory and practice of open and distance learning. These are not the proceedings of the conference but the papers do stem from ideas developed at the time. Most were drafted after the conference and have been substantially revised since then.

The title of the book emerged from our discovery that despite the advent of new technology and the sudden escalation of funding for 'open learning', the practice of open learning remained in general a limited expression of what is possible in theory. Our main thesis, which we develop in the commentaries introducing each section of the book and in the final chapter, is that distance teaching is not the only possible form of open learning, that in some ways distance teaching is not 'open', and that there is a great deal of room for the further development of other forms of open learning besides distance teaching.

In Section I, comprising Chapters 1 to 5, theoretical issues are addressed which set out possible approaches to open learning and identify a number of challenges and problems that need to be overcome in practice.

In Section II, comprising Chapters 6 and 7, recent technological advances are described that offer possibilities for open learning, and the limitations which remain are discussed.

In Section III, Chapters 8, 9 and 10 describe cases of distance teaching in Great Britain. Chapter 11 introduces and analyses three cases in mainland Europe.

The book will be of special interest for those who have a professional concern to open up opportunities for adults to learn and develop. It is for adult educators, for example, and management trainers, providers of professional, technical and other vocational education, and others in positions from which the policy and practice of open learning can be influenced. Although we cannot claim to offer tried and trusted techniques for going beyond distance teaching towards open learning, we hope to provide a framework within which practice can develop.

We offer many thanks to Don Binsted, Director of Distance Learning at the Department of Management Learning, University of Lancaster. Don's energy, enthusiasm and encouragement made the initial conference a success. Without him we would not have had the opportunity to do research into open learning and this book, part of our ongoing work in that area, would not have materialized.

We also thank those who were delegates and contributors to our conference but whose papers regrettably could not be included here.

Our thanks go to Michael Reynolds and Dai Hounsell for reading and commenting on parts of the book, and for encouraging us along the way. Our thanks go also to Sally Kington at SRHE for all the editorial work she did and to Christine Dytham and Susan Clarke for the help they gave us with preparing the manuscript.

We wish to acknowledge permission to quote from the following books and articles:

Child, J. (1977) *Organisation: A guide to problem and practice* London: Harper & Row

Clancey, W.J. (1984) Methodology for building an intelligent tutoring system. In Kintsch, W. Miller, J.R. and Polson, P.G. (Eds) *Methods and Tactics in Cognitive Science* Hillsdale, NJ: Lawrence Erlbaum

O'Hanlon, W. and Wilk, J. (1987) *Shifting Contexts* New York: Guildford Press

Open University (1980) *Health Choices* Community Education Course, The Open University

Roberts, D. (1984) Ways and means of reducing early student drop out rates *Distance Education 5* (1) 50–71 Darling Downs Institute Press for the Australian and South Pacific External Studies Association

Säljö, R. (1979) *Learning in the Learner's Perspective: II: Differences in Awareness* Reports from the Institute of Education, University of Goteberg, Sweden, No. 77

Smith, K.C. (1979) *External Studies at New England: A Silver Jubilee Review* Armidale: University of New England Press, Australia

Watzlawick, P. (1978) *The Language of Change* New York: Basic Books

Vivien Hodgson, Sarah Mann and Robin Snell
Department of Management Learning
University of Lancaster
July 1986

THE CONTRIBUTORS

TORE AKSJØBERG Norsk Korrespondanseskole, Norway

ANGIE BALLARD Institute of Educational Technology, Open University, UK

RICHARD L. BOOT Department of Management Learning, University of Lancaster, UK

MAGDOLNA CSATH Karl Marx University of Economic Sciences, Hungary

IAN CUNNINGHAM Ashridge Management College, UK

CHRIS ELGOOD Chris Elgood Associates, UK

ROBERT F. GRAHAM University of Strathclyde Business School, UK

ROBERT P. HARROWER University of Strathclyde Business School, UK

VIVIEN E. HODGSON Department of Management Learning, University of Lancaster, UK

CHRISTOPHER MABEY formerly of British Telecom Management College now with Rank Xerox, UK

SARAH J. MANN Department of Management Learning, University of Lancaster, UK

DENT M. RHODES Illinois State University, USA

HEINZ SCHWALBE Gesellschaft für Rational-kommunikation, West Germany

JOHN SELF Department of Computing, University of Lancaster, UK

ROBIN S. SNELL Department of Management Learning, University of Lancaster, UK

ALISON STRANG Institute of Education, University of London, UK

I
ISSUES
IN THEORY
AND
RESEARCH

COMMENTARY

In the first chapter in this first section, Richard Boot and Vivien Hodgson identify two basic orientations to open learning: a dissemination and a development orientation. Proponents of the first aim to open up access to knowledge and of the second to encourage an individual's self-actualization as a learner. Boot and Hodgson suggest that those with a dissemination orientation view knowledge as a commodity, assessed by experts who provide certification, and as facts and skills which exist independently of people but which can contribute to an individual's more effective achievement of work-related tasks. Increasing dissemination may entail the delegation by educators of most of the teaching to resource materials so that knowledge is always accessible to learners, regardless of time and place. Educators retain control of the expert task of assessing students' work and the moral task of ensuring that the syllabus remains relevant to requirements, whether vocational or academic.

Those with a development orientation have a radically different philosophy of education. The task of education becomes not one of transmitting knowledge from expert to learner and thence to the learner's job, but of developing the whole person and a capacity for independence of mind. Learners are encouraged to strive to make sense of themselves in the context of their world, including the world of their work.

Boot and Hodgson point out some of the defects both in the dissemination and the development orientation. Dissemination seems to imply a lack of opportunity for learners to make their own interpretations and choices. Development, as currently conceived, tends to have an élitist connotation, requiring the concentration of resources for the benefit of the few. Neither seems to embody the fullness of openness for individual sense-making or for access to development, although the best of both might achieve this.

It is Alison Strang in Chapter 3 who is most explicit about the direction that might be taken by a synthesis of the two orientations. Her starting point is to question how resources are currently used in implementing 'dissemination' strategies of open learning. Learners could use distance teaching materials as resources for development rather than as vehicles for the acquisition of predigested knowledge. She treats 'independence of mind' – a central theme in the development orientation- as an attitude that learners can take upon themselves whatever their context, once they have understood the concept. She suggests that there is nothing inherent in a dissemination orientation that precludes development. She does argue, however, that present teaching and publicity materials often convey the impression of *nothing more* than dissemination. Many learners do not themselves seem to be aware of the possibility of arriving at their own unique learning to suit their own unique vocational and developmental purposes.

Strang suggests that much could be achieved by removing the source of such perceptual and attitudinal barriers to development by inspecting publicity and teaching materials for messages which distort and limit the vision of what development can be. Her ideas are the more powerful for being made in the context of technical education, popularly conceived as a matter of remembering the nuts and bolts of things. That is her very point: whatever the subject matter, we can make it our own.

Strang may, however, be underestimating the scale of the barriers. The limitations on conceptions of learning that she refers to are constantly reinforced by our institutions and by teachers, and seem to be widely entrenched in our culture. Could it be that in order to synthesize open development and open dissemination all learners, prior to using distance teaching materials, should take part in the kind of development activity discussed by Ian Cunningham in Chapter 4? If so, we return to the question of making development opportunities and support for development more widespread.

Boot and Hodgson argue that if development is to be made available and acceptable as an educational process, a number of difficulties have first to be overcome. These include the role and structure of assessment within a development orientation, and the straightforward difficulty of a shortage of resources.

There is also the challenge of publicity. As Chris Elgood points out in Chapter 2, whatever the service offered, the image of it conveyed by the purveyor will be formative of expectation and will influence the level of desire for it. Those who have already commenced the process of development and who have some credibility in their organization or social circle could be a valuable source of honest testimonial. In publicity terms, the grapevine may work better than the mass media. An honest picture of development is likely to be a messy one, however, and may not square with current images of educational professionalism. We may need to reconstruct the concept of teacher professionalism to include the provision of good quality support for learner development.

The reality of learner development is, nonetheless, a difficult one. As Robin Snell suggests in Chapter 5, it can involve pain and struggle as well as joy. Texts and other materials are limited in how much they can on their own help the learner through such emotions. Other people are an inherent part of learner development, people with whom to share the challenge and collaborate in addressing one another's meanings and understandings. One way forward would be to ensure that such collaboration can be the case whoever you are and wherever you are.

1

Open Learning:
Meaning and Experience

Richard L. Boot and Vivien E. Hodgson

What is open learning? Various attempts at definition seem to revolve around the notion of freedom from constraints on the learning process. Typically, following Coffey (1977), such constraints are grouped as administrative (time, space, duration, cost, etc.) and educational (objectives, methods, sequencing, entry qualifications, assessment, etc.). Removing the former might be with the intention of increasing *logistical independence,* while removing the latter might be with the intention of encouraging *independence of mind.* But the removal of all of these constraints would in effect leave us with no educational provision at all. The issue, then, is less one of openness and more one of the extent to which formal educational provision has bounded learning. Indeed, perhaps we ought to use the term 'unbounded learning' in connection with such provision. This would at least acknowledge that learning and development are natural processes rather than things provided by educators. Unfortunately it still fails to acknowledge that for many people the organizations and institutions in which they live and work are the greatest source of constraint. In other words, while learning and development are *natural* processes, learning and development opportunities are not necessarily a *normal* part of everyday working life. The role of work organization, however, in enhancing or inhibiting learning is a separate — albeit related — issue, which we shall not pursue here.

A general feature in discussions of open learning at present is that it is predominantly seen from the perspective of the provider as though openness were solely a characteristic of the formal provision. We suggest here that it is also necessary to discuss the nature of the learning experience. This last point leads us on to another feature of current discussions of open learning. That is that they seem to concentrate on the 'open' part and leave 'learning' in the background, together with assumptions or beliefs about what it is and how it takes place.

We say 'current' discussions because we are aware of some tendency to talk of open learning as though it were a recent innovation in educational thinking.

One only has to look at the work of John Dewey and his followers to realize that this is not true, however. And for them the nature of learning was central. What is new is the large amount of funding available for work in this area. And this funding is, or is taken to be, predominently in support of open access, ie the removal of administrative constraints. It is perhaps not surprising, therefore, that consideration of learning has been left in the background. In this chapter we intend it to be in the foreground where it belongs. So we shall consider the links between assumptions about learning, educational provision, and the learning experience.

We shall perhaps be drawing the differences among the various assumptions about learning and the related intentions for open learning provision more starkly than is immediately apparent when comparing particular programmes. We do however believe them to be major differences, with a significant effect upon the learning experience.

Assumptions about Learning

Different assumptions about learning seem to be based upon different assumptions about the nature of knowledge. For some, knowledge can be conceived of as a (valuable) commodity which exists independently of people and as such can be stored and transmitted (sold). For others, knowledge, or more appropriately knowing, is best seen as a process of engaging with and attributing meaning to the world, including self in it. For the former, then, learning becomes a process of acquisition and addition of facts and skills. For the latter, learning is the elaboration and change of the meaning-making processes and the enhancement of personal competence.

Given those two sets of assumptions about knowledge and learning, it is not surprising to find different assumptions about the purpose of education. The purpose of education based on the first set of assumptions is the dissemination of stored knowledge, to make it available to those who lack it. The purpose of education based on the second set of assumptions is the development of the whole person, especially the continuing capacity to make sense of oneself and of the world in which one lives.

The Nature of the Provision

What do each of the above sets of assumptions imply for the nature of the provision for open learning? Regardless of the assumptions they are operating from, providers will have a number of concerns in common but the way they deal with them will be different. Both are likely to be designing for the 'independent' learner but independence is likely to have different meanings. For the one it implies individualization, with the resulting freedom to control the timing, pacing, location and so on of prescribed study. For the other it implies autonomy and the freedom to determine both the form and content of learning. In each case learner choice will be regarded as important. In the one however, it is likely to be on a 'cafeteria' basis: selecting from a set range of carefully prepared dishes. In the other it is likely to be on a 'self-catering' basis: planning menus, deciding what raw materials are required and experimenting with ways of preparing them. In the former the course structure is likely to be based on, or at least closely related to, the organization of the predetermined course materials, and a lot of consideration will be given to overcoming problems of application and transfer to the student's own working life. In the latter it is likely to be based upon the processes of planning, deciding and experimenting. Transfer as such will not be specifically catered for in that the participant's own working life will be regarded as the prime source of learning materials. In order to engage with the courses successfully, 'students' of the former are likely to be encouraged to improve their 'study skills' while 'participants' in the latter will be encouraged to 'learn to learn'. The importance attributed to the social element is also likely to differ. In the one, other people are likely to be seen as a source of moral support, encouragement and perhaps comparison for the individualized learning task. In the other they are likely to be regarded as an inherent part of the learning venture, providing challenge and collaboration in the construction of personal meaning.

There will also be difference in assumptions about the tutor's role. In one the tutor, as subject expert, will in effect be the guardian of knowledge and will have responsibility for teaching or instructing, although this may well be delegated to course media and materials. In the other the tutor will be a facilitator, resource person and co-learner. While acknowledging differences in role and possibly experience the tutor will not regard the meanings he/she attribute to events as any more valid than anyone else's. For the former, assessment is, in effect, a measure of proficiency against some externally-recognized standard and as expert the tutor is the best person to judge the quality of work. For the latter the concept of assessment is problematical. Some might argue that personal development can only be personally assessed. But it does not take place in a social vacuum, so some form of collaborative assessment against criteria mutually agreed between self, peers and tutor (which are likely to be different for each individual) is favoured. In this way it will be intended that assessment should form part of the learning process and not simply be a measure of learning achieved.

Taken together all these assumptions about learning and the educational provision deemed appropriate can be taken to represent two basic orientations to open learning. The former we shall call a *dissemination* orientation, and the latter a *development* orientation. The characteristics of each are summarized in Table 1.1.

So far we have only talked about the providers' orientations, but students or participants will have their own beliefs and assumptions about learning and how it comes about. They too are likely to come to any educational provision with either a dissemination or a development orientation influencing their expectations. We can probably assume that their expectations will correspond to those of the providers' who have a similar orientation. There may however be difficulties if students or participants find themselves on a course or programme based on assumptions they do not share, with an orientation that does not match their own. The question arises whether learning can ensue

	Dissemination	**Development**
ASSUMPTIONS ABOUT KNOWLEDGE	Knowledge as *valuable commodity* existing independently of people. Can be stored and transmitted	Knowing as *process* of engaging with and attributing meaning to the world, including self in it
ASSUMPTIONS ABOUT LEARNING	*Acquisition and addition* of facts, concepts and skills	*Elaboration and change* of the meaning-making processes. Enhancement of personal competence
PURPOSE OF EDUCATION	*Dissemination* of stored knowledge	*Development* of the whole person
MEANING OF INDEPENDENCE	*Individualization*	*Autonomy*
BASIS OF LEARNER CHOICE	*Cafeteria* Selection from a set range of carefully prepared dishes	*Self-catering* Planning menus, deciding raw materials required and experimenting with ways of preparing
COURSE STRUCTURE	*Based on syllabus* The organization and sequencing of course materials	*Based on processes* of planning, deciding and experimenting
CONCERNS FOR RELEVANCE	Consideration given to problems of *application and transfer*	Participants' *own working lives* regarded as prime source of *learning material*
TO ENGAGE SUCCESSFULLY WITH COURSE	Students encouraged to improve *study skills*	Participants encouraged to *learn to learn*
THE SOCIAL ELEMENT	Other people seen as source of *moral support*, encouragement and comparison for individualized learning task	Other people seen as *inherent part of learning* venture, providing challenge and collaboration in construction of personal meaning
TUTOR'S ROLE	*Subject expert* Guardian of knowledge. Responsible for teaching or instructing. May delegate to course media and materials	*Facilitator,* resource person and co-learner. Meanings he/she attributes to events no more valid than anyone else's
ASSESSMENT	Measure of proficiency against *externally recognized standard.* Tutor as subject expert best person to judge quality of work	Part of learning process. Based on *collaborative* assessment against *mutually agreed criteria*

Table 1.1
Two orientations to open learning

from both match and mismatch. We believe it probably can, but that students or participants will either have to adopt special strategies to cope with mismatch or be 'socialized' into the alternative orientation. Whatever happens, the nature of the experience is likely to differ according to match or mismatch.

Learning Experience

Having described the different assumptions made about learning and how these are reflected in the nature of the educational provision associated with open learning programmes, we should now like to look at the learning experience associated with two such programmes. We intend not so much to decide in what ways the two programmes can be described as open in terms of the distinctions we have identified as to examine in what ways they were experienced as open by the people taking part.

An outline of the stated aims, design and structure of the two programmes is given in Table 1.2. By using the distinctions described in the first part of the chapter as a framework for looking at people's experience of the two programmes, it is possible to get a clearer picture both of the ways in which each was experienced as open and of the problems and difficulties learners had with them.

Programme A

Participants in Programme A made special mention of its 'taking responsibility for your own learning' aspect, particularly in terms of learner choice, course structure, concerns for relevance and learning to learn. For example, as one learner explained:

> I feel I am starting to come to terms with the programme a bit now. When I was asked to choose a topic for the first seminar paper, I was completely flummoxed. Now I have more of an idea of what I want to do for my next piece of work because I'm beginning to see the value of how it fits with what I am doing at work.

This seems to be a reflection both of problems experienced with coming to terms with learner autonomy on the programme, and of a growing recognition of one's own working life as a source of learning material. In addition there is by inference report of being encouraged (forced) to make choices as well as to plan one's own learning. This learner elaborated on the latter aspect and her experience of it:

> I came with different ideas this time. A private agenda of things I would like to get positively from the workshop. I'd not done that previously. You need to have some expectation or an agenda or you get nothing out — yet you're still putting in a lot for other people — it should be a two way thing.

STATED AIM (from course literature)

A — An advanced development programme for experienced practitioners ... It aims to provide greater understanding of the processes which promote effective learning. Two principles on which programme is based:

(1) there should be close integration of the participants' theoretical and conceptual learning on the course with the continuing development of their own practice;
(2) participants should become increasingly able to take responsibility for the management of their own learning.

B — To improve individual managerial performance by combining sound theory with practical advice and exercises;
— major emphasis on what managers actually do and how they can improve performance.

WHO FOR

A — experienced practitioners in the fields of management education, training or development.

B — managers who wish to update their knowledge. Newly-appointed managers who want to enhance their employment opportunities.

DISTINCTIVE DESIGN FEATURES AND CHARACTERISTICS

A — Content of the programme loosely pre-specified in terms of broad topic areas;
— participants encouraged to take responsibility for managing their own learning;
— emphasis on support with no pre-designed learning materials.

B — Content of programme pre-specified and contained in pre-designed learning materials:
— participants expected to work their way through materials;
— emphasis on well presented materials, including video and audio cassettes as well as printed.

ASSESSMENT

A — Based on five pieces of coursework: three seminar papers, one project essay, one dissertation;
— topic of work self chosen; stated submission dates, but in practice flexible with end of programme being the final cut-off point; criteria for assessment reached by mutual agreement, with tutor being final arbiter.

B — Based on three pieces of coursework and an end of course exam;
— topic pre-set: stated submission dates, but in practice flexible with exam date being final cut-off point; criteria for assessment responsibility of tutor.

STRUCTURE OF PROGRAMME

A — Duration two years;
— four × five-day residential workshops;
— one × three-day residential workshop;
— one × two-day residential workshop;
— group tutorials every five to six weeks arranged by mutual agreement — usually one working day in duration.

B duration six months;
— structure of content also provided by course materials;
in addition
— three × $\frac{1}{2}$-day or evening tutorials (voluntary);
— one × two-and-a-half day residential workshop.

Table 1.2
Programmes A and B

In addition to her experience of planning, deciding and experimenting within the course structure, the learner is also referring here to her experience of the 'social element' of the programme. She talked further about such experiences:

> I'm approaching this piece of work quite differently from other pieces of work. I'm being less concerned about the outcome. I think before I wanted to have in my mind some kind of structural format to the way the thing would shape up or come out. At this stage with this one I'm not putting in any structure at all. Feels a bit risky but within my tutorial group and with my tutor it seems acceptable and after all if you don't try something new you won't find out if you can do it or not.

It seemed important to have the support and collaboration of the tutorial group to try something new and 'risky'. The collaborative, challenging aspect of the social element of the course is further demonstrated by another learner who described the tutorials as useful in terms of their role of '...gently just asking awkward questions which is really effective and really quite skilfully done, I found it effective.'

So far the descriptions of experience of the programme seem to reflect a development-orientation and at times, particularly early on in the programme, the fact that it was not necessarily easy to cope with or come to terms with. One gets the impression that part of the process of learning to learn on a development-oriented programme is developing or thinking through one's approach to the programme itself. This in turn is something which can be influenced and constrained by the learners' experience of assessment and the tutor role.

The learners' experience of assessment and the tutor role was not always what would be expected to be associated with a development-oriented programme. While the learner above spoke about the work she was doing for assessment in terms of personal development and in terms of self- and peer-assessment and the risks she was taking, other people's experience did at times reflect that which would more often be associated with a dissemination orientation. Thus one learner commented: 'I still have a problem with the assessment and what standard is required. For the first essay I just didn't know. Once we'd done that and got it back I felt a bit more sure.'

This 'external standard' experience of assessment was associated with the way in which some people perceived the tutor role. As one student succinctly put it, 'they do dish out the brownie points,' a fact which for some did contribute to their perceiving the tutors as authority figures who should be teaching or instructing them, not as resource persons and co-learners!

In summary then, Programme A was predominantly experienced as development-oriented. It is difficult, however, to determine the extent to which the problems participants encountered in taking responsibility for their own learning — which for some were exacerbated by their experience of assessment and the tutors' role — were the result of a mismatch of orientation or of the programme itself being a slightly mixed model.

Programme B

While many of the primary concerns of learners on Programme B were the same as those on Programme A, the way they were experienced was quite different. For example, much emphasis in Programme B was placed on how to engage successfully with the course, but very much more in terms of study skills than in Programme A and in having to select what parts of the course material to focus upon, particularly in relation to the assessed pieces of work. As one learner in Programme B explained:

> Book 7 took a long time. I put that down to maybe trying to get too much out of it. I don't know. I read every single word and tried to understand everything, whereas the advice you get from people is not to do that — if you are having a bit of difficulty, forget it, leave it or come back to it. Which is something in the early stages I wasn't prepared to do. Since then I have dropped full lessons sometimes. If it doesn't affect me currently, don't do it. There was a session on budgeting control, now I have no budgeting control and am not likely to have for a long time, so I can leave that and come back to it when it's appropriate because it is not necessary to do the assignment.

The social element of the course was experienced by many as being a very significant source of moral support and comparison between students as they in fact struggled to cover the course syllabus as fully as possible and do all the required assignments.

Another learner, for example, made the following comment about group meetings with fellow students on the course:

> Sometimes you might get, well, I tried X and it didn't work because of Y and we'd discuss that. I found them useful for that purpose. You can compare notes on what you are doing. Sometimes when you are talking together as a group some things come to light which you didn't appreciate, you'd missed a point or whatever. Also it has been useful, some of the sessions we have had to find out what other people are doing, where they are up to and what they are doing on the course.

There is also here a sense of seeing the course as an opportunity both to acquire facts, concepts and skills, and to apply these to one's work. Many people apparently experienced the tutor as the 'guardian of knowledge' and the source of confirmation of how things should be perceived. The first learner quoted above deferred, for example, to his tutor's view of the content of the course:

> I thought I knew what control meant but I wasn't too clear; maybe they attach a different meaning to control as far as it applies to management. They talk about control being a process of directing, rather than of helping to steer people along the right path, rather than in the sense of military control where people do exactly as they are told. I'm only able to say that to you because that's what the tutor said in the tutorial.

The same student had a high regard for the tutor's comments on his work as if he did indeed see the tutor as 'the best person to judge the quality of his work':

> I expected a good mark because I'd put a lot of effort into it but I was encouraged by the comments 'good assignment', 'keep up the good work'. He was complimentary in the report as well, although obviously he did pick up some things. I got the highest mark in the group. Makes you feel good.

This view of the tutor, particularly in relation to assessed work, was very prevalent amongst the learners on Programme B and seems to fit in with their experience of the programme generally as dissemination-oriented. For most this seemed appropriate.

For some it was not true, however. At least one person experienced the tutor's imposition of criteria in the assessment of his work as problematical:

> For the first assignment it was like when I was at school — very good but I hadn't answered the question. He said it was a 4 out of 5 but gave me 4 out of 10 because I hadn't answered the question. I felt I had a grasp of the course, which I had demonstrated in answering the question. I felt there were areas he had marked me down on which had nothing to do with the course — it was just a matter of what he wanted me to be saying; whereas I felt I didn't need to be relating everything to the course.

Here there seems to be a mismatch in orientations. The learner is clearly reluctant to accept the tutor's judgement as 'the best'. On the other hand most learners on the programme had no such problem. Their biggest problem was in trying to do everything that was demanded of them by the course structure in a way that would satisfy some externally laid down standard. Those who were able to achieve this, in point of fact, experienced the programme as an extremely valuable and useful one!

Issues and Implications

We have attempted to show that it is possible to distinguish both the provision and the experience of different open learning programmes according to their basic orientation — dissemination or development — and to distinguish the students' orientations too. But what are the implications of such distinctions?

Let us start by examining the issue of mismatch between programme orientation and student orientation and how providers should respond to it. One option obviously is to do nothing, and hope that students will gain benefit from involvement in the programme either by adopting appropriate coping strategies or by being 'adequately' socialized. If neither happens it can be regarded simply as bad luck or, more cynically, can be accounted for by labelling the unlucky individuals as poor or problem students. Such a response would seem to be suspect in terms of openness, whether seen from a dissemination or a development point of view.

Providers could attempt to obviate mismatch before programmes begin by actively selecting for match. But even assuming that the difficulties of assessing for true orientation could be overcome, decreasing openness would result from increasing barriers to access. And it is not clear whether tackling the problem via the promotion and marketing of the programmes would bring any improvement either. That would involve statements about intentions, design, process, underlying assumptions and likely experience being made as fully, clearly and unambiguously as possible, and potential students knowing exactly what they would be letting themselves in for. They could thus be in a position to decide for themselves whether to undertake the programme or not. It is doubtful, however, whether it is possible to convey the true nature of the experience to those who have experienced nothing similar, a problem attached particularly to development-orientated programmes in that, in the UK at least, educational provision is predominantly dissemination-oriented. In any case it is debatable whether selection by engineering self-selection genuinely results in more open access.

So far we have been talking about mismatch as though it only occurred between students and programmes. But there are related problems for tutors. It is not only a question of alignment of value orientations: each type of programme requires its own range of skills and competences. For the reasons mentioned earlier it is likely that tutors will have had more opportunity for developing those appropriate to the dissemination-orientation than to the development-orientation. In addition, if they are located in an educational institution they may well experience pressure to operate in a dissemination mode or at least to 'justify' deviating from the 'normal' mode. This is likely to be most evident in connection with assessment. It is clear from the two programmes cited above that once assessment is involved it has a powerful effect on the way the programme is experienced, whatever its orientation. Attempts to introduce some form of self- and peer-assessment, in a context in which assessment is primarily seen as a measure of proficiency against some absolute externally-recognized standard, can result in a compromise procedure which gives students rather mixed messages. This may be what underlies the experiences reported by some of the students on Programme A.

So far, implicit in what we have been saying is the assumption that the two orientations are incompatible. But is this inevitably so? Could it be that they simply serve different purposes and perform different functions in the common quest for openness? One way of trying to answer such questions would be to look at their respective advantages and disadvantages in this respect.

The essence of the dissemination orientation is open access. It centres on the preparation and packaging of materials in a form that will enable widespread availability for individualized study, free from administrative constraints. In comparison with this the development orientation could reinforce a kind of educational élitism. Firstly, since the appropriateness of materials and other resources cannot be pre-specified, the development orientation is dependent upon access to a rich resource reservoir; and secondly, as this orientation is currently conceived, face-to-face interaction between participants and between participants and tutors is a central component, which miligates against large numbers being involved on any one programme, and so represents a constraint on access.

Set against this, the essence of the development orientation is open curriculum, if that is not a contradiction in terms. It centres on the provision of structures and processes to enable individuals to control the direction and content of their own learning, and to support them in the creation and validation of their own meanings. By comparison the dissemination orientation, with its emphasis on the acquisition of preconstructed knowledge and movement toward predetermined ends, can result in individuals being deprived of the freedom to become their own meaning-makers.

The challenge facing all those genuinely interested in fully open learning is: 'Is it possible to combine the best of both orientations?' We are not sure what an educational provision based upon 'developmental dissemination' would look like, but we do believe it is worth working towards.

2

Motivating Learners

Chris Elgood

The suggestions made in this chapter about the design of distance learning materials are drawn from extensive experience of the creation and conduct of management games and from pursuit of a higher degree through part-time research. That combination of circumstances offered me an opportunity to make connections between accepted theory and successful practical actions.

My suggestions have to do with providing motivational support for the learner. They are not set out in perfect order, because in some cases the connections between them are essentially logical while in other cases two different concepts emerged by chance from one historical event and are not sequentially connected. There is also some degree of overlap. This happens when one suggestion is based on the exploration of an academic idea and another results from scanning the commercial world: the ideas are formulated in different words, but on reflection one sees that they are saying much the same thing. I have not attempted to eradicate such duplication, for the way in which different sources reinforce each other is quite illuminating.

My experience is in the design of packages that are used by persons other than the designer, so it might be thought that the relevance to distance learning lies in that element of geographical separation. That is only the case in part, for while some of the games involved can be used directly by a student, most of them require the presence of a tutor or administrator. The relevance to distance learning comes rather from the psychological freedom that such games offer the student, including the freedom (even the temptation) to deny their value and take mental leave of absence. As with distance learning, this psychological freedom to disengage makes student motivation an important consideration.

Management games are in general poorly defined, and I use the term widely here. I include some things that might elsewhere be called 'structured experiences' and others that might be called 'business simulations'. The essential common feature is that they should be contrived situations, artificial environments from which the designer believes that students can learn. Learning may take place in two ways. First, the games can call for decisions, which have 'better' or 'worse' outcomes depending on the belief of the designer about how the real world behaves. The hope is that the direct and personal experience of making an imperfect or wrong decision will provide the students with a deeper and more lasting form of learning than would come from direct instruction. The danger attached to this view is that students who consider the contrived situation to be invalid will also deem any potential implications for their own decision-making to be invalid.

Secondly, management games can touch on the personal behaviour and attitudes of the students, and learning in this area is, I feel, especially dependent on reflection after the event. Thus if the event is 'written off' at an early stage then the chances of the student reflecting upon it will be reduced, and consequently the chances of learning also. From the designer's point of view the maintenance of motivation and commitment to participate in the game and reflect on it afterwards is essential.

The likeness to distance learning may not yet seem to be sufficiently established. For instance, it is quite obvious that the distance learner, temporarily bored or annoyed with what the text has to say, may give it up and go out to play golf or whatever. This is not what one would expect where students are together in some formal environment and there is a tutor present. The following points, however, illustrate certain characteristics of management games which make them relevant to distance learning:

1 In setting up a contrived learning activity like a management game tutors step outside the conventional boundaries of their role and commit themselves to communication through an instrument. If they believe that it has some value they will leave it to work in the hoped-for manner without attempting to reclaim the initiative. Also, the students in these circumstances will normally be divided into small groups and the tutor cannot be present with all of them.

2 Most management games rely in part on mistakes made by the students. They contain a number of contrived pitfalls. Not everybody enjoys being tested in this way, and to some the very prospect of taking part in such an event is demotivating.

3 The tutors who run management games are frequently committed to the idea that real learning can come only from constructive commitment to the process by the learner. They feel that too much intervention by them will increase student dependence and shift the responsibility for learning away from the learner and back to the authority figure. They therefore refrain from using their position to extort the appearance of commitment.

Thus the tutor using these methods of management education has reduced control of the situation, and the student has greater potential freedom than would be the case with wholly conventional methods. These are also characteristics of distance learning. One should not be seduced by the fact of geographical separation into believing that distance learning is totally unlike anything else. I believe that a number of ideas which I have developed for encouraging and maintaining motivation in management games are equally applicable in the design of distance learning programmes.

Motivation through Early Action

The idea of motivating students by giving them an early opportunity to take action emerged when time was at a premium. The games concerned were of the type that seek to model the economic behaviour of a business, and are full of instructions about how particular figures must be handled. They sometimes also include a variety of complex forms that have to be understood and completed. Such games normally have written instructions for the players, but the temptation for tutors is to improve on the instructions by mastering the procedures themselves and explaining them. The result, after numerous trials, seemed to be that the players still needed to read the instructions and still took just as long to do so. The only effect of the tutors 'improvements' was to push the whole process backwards in time. There still remained a critical moment when individual players strove to implement the instructions and asked questions when they found themselves stuck. Real understanding only emerged when the experience of trying to play caused them to formulate specific questions and look for specific, usable answers. The conclusion I drew from this was that formal introduction should be minimal, and 'in-game' assistance maximal.

How does this relate to distance learning? There are obvious problems in the lack of opportunity for the learner to ask questions, but is there perhaps a temptation for the designer to make similar assumptions about the need to explain? One can logically argue that students must be presented with all the necessary knowledge before they are required to use it. And who knows what is necessary and what is not better than the subject expert? But subject experts cannot know the extent of their students' present expertise, nor can experts know to what extent their own explanations are actually confusing the reader by creating conflicts with ideas already possessed. So perhaps there is a case for inviting 'action attempts' (possibly a choice of them) at an early stage — even before the necessary knowledge has theoretically been communicated in full. This would allow for the intuitive leap that is so satisfying when it proves to be correct. Answers could be provided to these action attempts, the facts about which attempts were made and whether they were successful being used to direct attention to those parts of the original explanation which were weak. Applications of the idea would differ dramatically, but the appeal being made to the designer is not to give in to the psychological compulsion to feel that you must always offer complete and perfect instruction before requiring action from the student. Perfection is a non-attainable ideal, and there are other forces to consider besides intellectual elegance.

Clarifying Intentions

It is reasonable for somebody engaged in the education and development of adults to make the general assumption that most students are motivated to learn. 'Why else did they enrol?' But that motivation does not drive them with equal force through all the stages of a programme, and there will be times when it needs to be supplemented. When students are tired and depressed, are doing badly, and see completion of the programme as impossible then expectancy theory (see, for example, Vroom 1964) tells us that despite a general desire to succeed motivation will be low. Zero times one hundred is zero!

So there is a need to consider what might be called 'immediate motivation' and to think in quite precise terms. After all, what does 'learning' really mean? We have ways of showing that a person has learnt, and we can identify behaviours that seem to aid learning, but we have difficulty in describing the learning process within the individual mind. A person saying 'I want to learn' must then expect, in terms of activities, instructions like: 'Read this book. Kick that ball. Pull this lever. Talk to those people.' But these do not encapsulate the learning process. In his chapter on 'Experience and Thinking' John Dewey (1916) writes:

> Mere activity does not constitute experience. It is dispersive, centrifugal, dissipating. Experience as trying involves change, but change is meaningless transition unless it is consciously connected with the return wave of consequences which flow from it. When an activity is continued into the undergoing of consequences, when the change made by action is reflected back into a change made by us, the mere flux is loaded with significance. We learn something.

This is an early identification in the learning process of two aspects — the undergoing of an experience and the mental activity of reflecting upon it and, perhaps, attaching meaning to it.

Reading *Democracy and Education* by John Dewey was one of the early benefits I experienced through my involvement in doing a research degree, and it was close in time to the opportunity to conduct a management game for the Executive Club in the head office of a large supermarket chain. The club was a quasi-official affair, and they wanted to vary the conventional format of weekly lectures by running a voluntary and competitive management game. The game was conducted by post, handling one decision each week, and to the surprise of the organizers twenty-eight of the original entry of thirty-two teams were still competing at the end. My initial expectation had been that the difficulties of getting together, and the disappointment of a few poor results, would cause a larger number to give up. At the end, I was allowed to administer a short questionnaire to the players which included the question: 'What kept you going for ten weeks?' Without any intention to do so, and without fully appreciating it, in posing that question I made a distinction between the activity of taking part and the process of reflection. In the course of my own reflective process it became clear to me that one could look at these two component parts of learning separately, and ask whether at this moment, it is a matter of persuading students to take part in the activity or to reflect on what has happened. It may be that the ways in which one offers motivation towards these two halves of the process are different. Hence the exhortation to think precisely about what it is that one seeks to motivate a person to do.

The Motivating Forces

Not long after the commercial activity of the Executive Club Game, I was able to mount an experiment at the University of Lancaster in furtherance of the research project. The idea behind it was the possibility of viewing activity and reflection separately and the immediate intention was to explore the different methods of presenting games. Are some formats of presentation more or less attractive than others? If they were, then would it follow that there were positive things one ought to do to encourage people to take part and de-motivators that one should avoid, since they might prejudice people against the event? The experiment was based on a single game design following a 'Treasure Hunt' model that required participants to analyse the clues in detail. Three outward formats were presented, and participants were shown the layout of the room, with the impedimenta in place. They were asked for their immediate reactions to being asked to take part with others in the game for which the room had been prepared. The three different formats in which the clues were offered were:

— interrogating a computer;
— lifting coloured counters from a hole to see what colour lay underneath;
— adding together numbers (each player having one digit) to get the identity of a particular clue.

The responses seemed to suggest that:

— interest, disinterest or rejection were not related to the artefacts themselves and their appearance, but to the ways in which respondents perceived them, and to the parallel situations that were evoked in their minds;
— many of the reactions were prompted by concern for the respondent's likely image in the eyes of others who might be taking part. The artefacts and formats seemed to be creating expectations about a social situation in which the respondent might 'look good' or 'look bad'.

The idea that the game was a social situation linked back to the questionnaire about the Executive Club Game, where the reasons given for keeping going for ten weeks were quite often concerned with loyalty to colleagues or the loss of self-respect that might follow from giving up.

All of this was surprising to a researcher pre-conditioned to see the desire to learn as the prime motivator when involvement in an alleged learning experience was concerned. Apparently that motivation could be overshadowed by other forces, some of which were not related to learning at all. It became possible to imagine a person judging a learning experience by reference to the social rewards or social penalties that it seemed to offer. The question arose: 'If motivation to learn is not paramount, then what other motivations are in operation?'; and that led me on to ask: 'What other motivations are there? I was back to considering human motivation in general, and asking what is known about it.

The broader the context in which a question is framed, the more one can see similarities with other fields. Three apparently different lines of inquiry seemed now to have something in common. My research persona was asking: 'What causes people to become interested?' The commercial persona was subconsciously asking the marketing question: 'What is the benefit that I can use to persuade people to buy?' The student persona was asking: 'What is known about motivation?' I found a number of ideas in the literature which illuminated my thinking about each of these questions. I discuss them below.

Ideas from Classical Social Psychology

By considering a distance learning course simply as a task requiring motivation, I have derived the following suggestions from classical social psychology:

i   offer the student an awareness of having made progress;

ii   try to provide a continuing and escalating experience of success;

iii   give recognition of the merits of the work, even where the outcome is imperfect;

iv   recognize the personal identity of the individual students, and their circumstances;

v   allow the students some freedom in the order in which they tackle their assignments;

vi   make sure that they know beforehand where the bit that currently seems a mystery is going to fit into the whole subject.

The first four suggestions stem from the view that man is a wanting animal, and if something proves interesting, desirable, or motivating, it does so because of the perceived rewards or benefits or satisfactions that are attached to it in an individual's mind. Who has had something significant to say about that? A.H. Maslow has. The upper sections of Maslow's (1943) hierarchy of needs deal with Love, Esteem and Self-Actualization. Amongst the words he uses to characterize love and esteem, and the circumstances promoting them, are: friends, affectionate relationships with people in general, a place in one's group, high evaluation of ourselves, the esteem of others, adequacy, recognition, attention and appreciation. In his summary of esteem needs Maslow writes: 'Satisfaction of the esteem needs leads to feelings of self-confidence, worth, strength, capability and adequacy of being useful and necessary in the world.' According to Maslow these are the things that people want, once the more basic physiological and security needs have been satisfied. He suggests that they can be gratified either by some response from another person or by some change in circumstances that leads to the belief that such a response will be forthcoming. The first four suggestions above are thus direct attempts to apply the ideas that Maslow offers concerning love and esteem.

A quite reasonable response to the first two suggestions might be: 'I do those anyway.' For example, any competent creator of programmed learning packages would seek to promote and encourage successful responses and to offer the material in graded steps.

It is, however, necessary to emphasize the rather subtle point that motivation does not have to be directly related to the acknowledged object of learning. One can and should distinguish between the impact of an event on students' knowledge and the impact on their attitudes. It may happen that some feature of the programme adds nothing at all to knowledge or skill, but does provide enjoyment and does cause students to see their involvement in the programme in a more favourable light. It may also increase their propensity to reflect upon the programme, and cause them to achieve insights that they would otherwise have missed. Many school teachers will be aware how sharing in the interests of pupils, even if those interests are unconnected with the subject of study, can gradually alter the pupils' attitudes to the subject of study itself. The pupils experience acknowledgement of themselves as individuals and a favourable reaction to their own knowledge and skill. The good feelings (or rewards) that these things represent become associated with the formal subject of study.

The last two suggestions were inspired by *Alienation and Freedom* by Robert Blauner (1964). Of course, his book is sub-titled 'The Factory Worker and his Industry', and we are not here concerned with factory workers. But a factory worker is just a human being in one sort of job rather than another, and it seems quite reasonable to explore the possibility that the circumstances that alienate or satisfy a human being in one environment have their counterparts in another. When he described the things that people find unattractive in work, Blauner also gave some attention to their opposites:

The opposite of powerlessness is ... the state of freedom and control.

By this he means not being dominated by the work that has been set, but having freedom to make one's own decisions about how one tackles it.

The opposite of meaninglessness ... is understanding of a life plan or of an organisation's total functioning and activity.

That is to say, knowing what it is all about and where each piece that one is engaged upon fits in with the whole.

Are not some educators just as guilty as some managers and some work engineers of making restrictive unilateral decisions about the 'right' order in which certain things should be done, and about the degree of freedom to be allowed to the person actually doing the work and the degree of explanation that is in order?

Ideas from Marketing and Advertising

Three suggestions derive from the commercial world:

i   try to suggest that by taking part in the activity the student will be in excellent company, will be demonstrating sterling personal qualities and acquiring an enviable battery of skills;

ii　design the material in such a way that the students are conscious of
testing and increasing their skills;

iii　present the material in such a way that it conveys a professional quality
and a general feeling of up-marketness.

It was the idea that one could make a distinction between an activity and
reflection on that activity which first suggested a look at advertising. For the
specialists in that area have only seconds of an observer's time in which to
operate and arouse enough interest to trigger a trial of the product or service.
In her book *Decoding Advertisements*, Judith Williamson (1978) seeks to analyse
the ways in which specific visual advertisements achieve their effect. She
examines some that are in a competitive situation where there is really not
much to choose between the practical effects of the different products. One is
as good as the other. One of the advertisers' tricks in that case is to link the
product to particular individuals who are admired by their target population
or who possess qualities that the target population values. The idea is that by
purchasing and using the product the customer becomes 'like such-and-such a
person', or 'one such-and-such a group'. The precise source of motivation
being used is not a fact but a feeling. Taking soap as an example, customers
are not going to be any healthier or cleaner by buying one soap rather than
another, but they may feel satisfaction from a sense of identity with all the
marvellous and prestigious people who (allegedly) also use it. Is this not an
application of the motivators described by Maslow as 'high evaluation of self'
and 'the esteem of others'? This would suggest that the ideas originating in
one set of circumstances can be successfully put to work in another. For
advertising certainly works.

The trade publication *Campaign* (September 1984) carried a 'Special Report
on Premiums and Incentives' which was all about promotional games for
service station forecourts. The writers were prepared to make experience-
based statements about the characteristics a game must have if it were to catch
the public imagination. They mentioned excitement, of course, which has to
be linked to the possibility of winning a substantial prize, but they also argued
that there must be some way in which the players can test or prove or increase
their skill or knowledge, for satisfaction is found in so doing. Does this not link
up with the words like 'capability' and 'adequacy' that Maslow uses? The
inference is that feelings of 'having done well' and 'having succeeded' are
motivators readily available for use.

I had a pleasant shock when getting substantial favourable feedback about a
new brochure. It had been prepared by a professional consultant who
previously knew nothing about the products and services being offered, and
whose suggestions differed markedly from all previous attempts. In a normal
A4 format the front page carried nine words in all, the rest being a plain white
background for a simple but attractive abstract design. The explanation seems
to be that the purpose of a first impression is to convey a feeling of quality and
confidence rather than to offer detail. That comes later on when the potential
user has formed the impression of a supplier 'who seems to know what he is
doing'. There may be a valuable lesson here for educators. Such people are
conditioned to see the written word as the prime communicative medium, but

that is a rather simplistic view. The experts in marketing and advertising are able to show us that in 'the open market' — as opposed to inside the walls of an educational institution — there are some circumstances in which some messages can be better or more quickly communicated by good design or even by clever packaging. This is especially true when the thing to be conveyed is an emotional feeling.

Overcoming Restrictions

The suggestion made here is that those who create distance learning material will probably have their roots in the educational world and may, unknowingly, have beliefs about what may or may not be done, and what is or is not respectable, that limit their options and are not really appropriate to the work in hand.

One such belief may be that the pursuit of knowledge is somehow demeaned if any use is made of 'lower' motivating factors to encourage students to learn. Yet such factors do already play a part in academic life and are explicitly recognized by various attendance regulations and other forms of compulsion. Because educators can so readily draw upon compulsion as a device, they have paid rather less attention to incentives. But incentives still operate, even though they are seldom noticed and never referred to. If one considers the benefits attaching to a lecture, the following incentives can certainly be cited:

— *Peace and security*   For about one hour nothing unforeseen can happen to students. The telephone cannot disturb them. Callers cannot visit them. They will be warm (in most institutions) and they can even go to sleep.
— *Maintaining group membership*   Students are visibly present in their peer group, attending an institutionally approved activity.
— *Relief*   Attending a formal lecture is an acceptable excuse for not doing something else.
— *Social gain*   The student can arrange to sit with particular people whose friendship is sought.
— *Prominence*   By asking questions, students can draw favourable attention to themselves and score points with the staff.

Consider also the matter of evening classes. One can imagine a scenario in which one spouse (Z) upbraids the other (X) for lack of ambition, and spouse X then enrolls at the technical college. Spouse X sleeps through the lectures and spends several hours drinking with fellow students before returning home. The project has met the physiological needs of spouse X (sleep and beer), the security needs of spouse X (no longer worried by criticisms of spouse Z) and the social needs of spouse X (convivial company).

So the point is that if the minor and immediate motivators are already operating within the conventional situation, what value is there in the argument that learning is somehow demeaned by considering them?

The other powerful argument for casting aside all restrictions originating in traditional educational values is that distance learning really does take the purveyor of knowledge into the open market. Most other formal educational activities have some of the advantages of a rigid schedule which provides the student with a discipline (often welcomed) and helps with the planning of time. After all, if a lecture is not going to be repeated there is a powerful argument for hearing it. With distance learning, the project is competing at every stage with other demands on learners: not just demands on their capacity as learners but on their total capacity as human beings. It is essentially a competitive situation, which makes the insights derived from the commercial world so important, and if designers of learning materials do not recognize this they will be at a disadvantage.

How can some of the ideas raised in this chapter be put into practice? One recommendation at the policy level is that every team concerned with distance learning material should have one member whose experience is primarily in marketing or with media. Detailed suggestions concerning package design might very well emerge from a formal brainstorming session with its established rule that nothing may be immediately ruled out. This is critical, because useful suggestions are likely to be controversial and there will always be immediately obvious reasons for rejecting them. But at the later stages of brainstorming supplementary ideas may crop up that make those originally seen as quite impossible just worth trying. Suggestions made outside that climate are dangerous, but how about something in the text that recognizes the isolation (from the rest of the family) that distance learning so often produces? Something that attaches to the task some sort of partner-inclusive element? Perhaps there might be a competition of which one part was course-related and could only be done by the student. A second part would not be course-related and would, by the rules, have to be done by some other person, previously named by the student. One can think of all sorts of reasons for not doing this, but that is the core of the whole argument: that as long as we continue to regard things as unacceptable we shall deny ourselves the experience that comes from trying. Can we not do some learning ourselves?

3

The Hidden Barriers

Alison Strang

In the development of open learning many of us have set ourselves the task of removing any barriers that inhibit effective learning. We are attempting to make learning more accessible in some ill-defined sense. How exactly do we decide what it is that deserves the attention of our enthusiastic demolition work?

Some so-called barriers may seem obvious, such as insistence on full-time study, or on a particular place of study which all students must attend. Others are not so clear — for example, hidden messages in the way a course is publicized. Ultimately the kinds of phenomena that we identify as inhibitory to learning will depend on the model of learning which underlies our thinking. Different models of learning entail different sets of barriers. There my starting point here is to discuss alternative models of the learning process. Before you read on, why not identify how you would try to describe or define learning?

Most models of learning can be characterized as either teacher-centred, process-centred or person-centred. The teacher-centred model implies that teachers (or the teaching material) are the source of knowledge. Successful learning will take place if students receive knowledge from the teachers. The model alerts us to the physical and psychological barriers which might lie between teachers and students and in some way prevent the knowledge from getting through. For example Carroll's model (1963) gives particular emphasis to quality and quantity of instruction. Bennett (1978), although not concentrating on teacher behaviour, proposes that quantity of schooling time and total active learning time are major variables. The teacher-centred model suggests that, in providing learning opportunities that are open to the students, there may be a concern to make sure that learning is available at a 'time, place and pace' convenient to them. Here learning is essentially an end result or product. It is the acquisition of knowledge by students.

In a process-centred model, learning is seen as the process by which students achieve results. Attention is focused on the students' performance of the learning process. Thus, it is recognized that it is the learners' approaches to studying that may create barriers to effective learning. The study skills training movement has its roots in this model of learning (Dansereau et al. 1979; Brown, Campione and Day 1981). Learners are taught how to learn, how to perform the various skills of study such as note taking or essay writing or managing their time. Distance education has led the way in promoting and developing study skills advice and training.

Yet the results of study skills training have been disappointing. Often those students most helped by it have been the ones who were already the more effective learners (Hills 1979); Elton et al. 1979). The work of both Graham Gibbs (1981) and Laurie Thomas and Harri-Augstein (1977) would suggest that it is not enough simply to teach skills or tell learners about more effective study methods. Becoming an effective learner involves fundamental changes in the whole person and one's attitude to learning. The process-centred model does not highlight attitudes to learning as potential barriers. It entails a view of the learner as a processor — which is fundamentally a mechanistic model.

A person-centred model of learning focuses attention on the students as human beings. Rather than considering them solely as learning machines the model encourages recognition of qualities such as the propensity to adopt attitudes, to have intentions, and to make decisions (Rogers 1983). By implication the model also suggests that it is in these very qualities that barriers to teaching may reside.

It is with the person-centred model of learning in mind that we have set about the work described in this chapter. As a research team, Eileen Sagar and I have been concerned with open learning in the context of the 'Open Tech' set up by the Manpower Services Commission. Our brief has been to investigate effective learning at a technician level within the Open Tech, with a view to developing guidelines for design. We have been working with a number of Open Tech projects, all of which are primarily aimed at a technician level student population, and cover general engineering subjects. Some are managed by further education colleges; others by employers' associations.

Here we are discussing issues arising from research which is still under way. We are not seeking to publish 'results' or 'findings', but are taking the opportunity to put forward some ideas as part of the process of their formulation.

We have been faced with the task of identifying the barriers which inhibit effective learning at technican level, and as we have said it is the person-centred model of learning that has guided our thinking. This is the model that acknowledges that learners are not machines but human beings whose actions are guided by their own decisions and intentions. It follows that an important key to understanding the learners' actions will be an understanding of the intentions and decisions which have led to them. Therefore our starting point in this research has been to find out about learners' goals, that is, their reasons for studying. If we can relate goals to actions, whether successful or unsuccessful in outcome, we may begin to uncover some of the hidden barriers to effective learning.

Why Students study

In interpreting Open Tech students' reasons for studying, we have followed the work of Elizabeth Taylor and the Open University Study Methods Group (Taylor et al. 1981). Taylor originally worked with university students at Surrey (1984) where she developed a system for classifying their reasons for studying. These she calls their 'orientations'.

Orientation	Interest	Aim	Concerns
VOCATIONAL	Intrinsic	Training	Relevance of course to career
	Extrinsic	Qualification	Recognition of worth of qualification
ACADEMIC	Intrinsic	Follow intellectual interest	Room to choose work, stimulating lectures
	Extrinsic	Educational advance	Grades, academic progress
PERSONAL	Intrinsic	Self-improvement	Challenge, interesting material
	Extrinsic	Proof of capability	Feedback, passing course
SOCIAL	Extrinsic	Have a good time	Facilities for sport and social activities

Table 3.1
Orientation and student concerns

As Table 3.1 illustrates, four main types of orientation were identified. 'Vocational', which concerns a current or future job; 'academic', which is to do with studying or education per se; 'personal', which concerns development as a person; and finally 'social', which can be summed up as the 'desire to have a good time'.

Each category could be further divided into sub-groups distinguishing between intrinsic and extrinsic interest in the course. So, for example, students who feel that they '... need the extra *know-how* to cope with the job,' would be expressing a 'vocational intrinsic' (Vi) orientation. They are actually interested in the content of the course because it will help them perform better at work. In contrast, others might express a 'vocational extrinsic' (Ve) orientation by saying: 'I need to get this certificate to have any hope of promotion.' Here the students' interest is in the certificate, not in the course content for its own sake.

However, Taylor's work has focused on undergraduates as students (Taylor et al. 1981) whereas our interest is in technicians as students. So we first conducted a small pilot study to discover the orientations of technician level students and see if Taylor's system would apply to them too. We found that it was indeed a useful and meaningful way of classifying technician students' reasons for studying. Although each one had various reasons for studying, on the whole their main reasons were vocational, as would be expected in this type of course. Secondary reasons fell into all the other categories except 'social', which was again unsurprising as these particular students were following a distance learning course and so were isolated from other students.

The pilot study was followed up by another, in which we took sixteen Open Tech students all studying at the same level on a particular course. By interview we elicited from them as many of their reasons for studying as possible, and asked them to identify their main one. Although on that occasion we were not able to take our own measure of learning outcome, a performance measure was available in the form of the results of a recent test taken as part of normal course assessment.

Once again, the students' reasons for studying were predominantly vocational; they were hoping that doing the course would help them in their job in some way. A comparison of orientations with performance on the assessment test (Table 3.2) revealed an important difference between students whose primary interest in the course was extrinsic (Ve) and those whose interest was intrinsic (Vi).

	Grades A/B	Grades C/D
VOCATIONAL — EXTRINSIC	1	7
VOCATIONAL — INTRINSIC	6	2

Table 3.2

Students' orientations & performance on course assessment.

As the table shows, there is a tendency for students with a Vi interest in the content to perform better on normal course assessment than those with a Ve interest. In this sample, the boundaries of the two groups overlapped to some extent with the distinction: 'blue collar' v. 'white collar' employees, and also with the distinction between those who had and those who had not volunteered to undertake the training. Conventional wisdom would expect both of these factors to relate to performance on course assessment: the 'blue collar'/'white collar' distinction because of its links with educational level, and voluntary participation because of its implications for motivation. Therefore it is particularly interesting to note that it was the distinction between Vi and Ve interest which seemed to have the strongest relationship with performance on course assessment.

By using Taylor's approach we are able to go beyond simple quantification of students' motivation. Taylor has demonstrated that each different orientation has specific implications for the sort of concerns which the student will have in studying. A closer inspection of the characteristics of students' orientations will throw light on this.

In our study, some students with a vocational orientation expressed an interest which was extrinsic to the content of the course. For example, one said: 'They said it would look good on my records ... enrolling on this course;' and another: 'I wanted to complete my qualifications.'

Such students might be quite strongly motivated to participate. However, given these aspects of their orientation, it is probable that their concern will largely be to fulfil the minimum requirements for staying on the course and passing the exams. In fact it is possible that simply being enrolled, and not passing exams, would be sufficient goal for the first student. We would not expect such concerns in themselves to promote effective learning. Some students' reasons for study might even inhibit learning. A number we interviewed mentioned that: 'I have been told that I will need these certificates if I'm to remain in my present grade in the future.' Some of these clearly resented the fact that they were being required to study to prove that they were capable of a job which they had been doing for years. The fear of failure and the anxiety likely to occur in that situation are known to have a very adverse affect on learning (Sarason 1975).

In contrast, students with a Vi orientation to the course tended to feel that studying was an opportunity to 'broaden my knowledge of the job' or 'sit back a bit ... you've no time to think on the job.' These students genuinely felt that the content of the course would be of interest to them and equip them better for their work. By looking at some of the examples of specific reasons, we may begin to see what goals will help students learn. One hoped that studying would '... help me in dealing with people when I have to take parents (of apprentices) and other visitors on factory tours.' Such students may be concerned to find out about aspects of the work on their factory which they currently have difficulty in explaining. As they look at the study materials they relate them to the particular practical situation they have in mind.

Another student pointed out that: 'The notes I make from the book will make perfect notes for explaining things to a client.' Perception of the very direct practical relevance of their studies should help such students to recognize the salient points in the materials, and evaluate the effectiveness of their notes for their own purposes.

As we have said, students have a complex combination of reasons for studying. Many whom we interviewed had strong secondary reasons that were not vocational. For example, one said: 'I suppose I've just got a personal wish to know,' which seems to fit in with Taylor's 'academic intrinsic' category, and thus with a concern to have control over the choice of topics to study. Quite a number had a significant personal orientation to their studying, seeing it as an opportunity for self-development. They expressed views such as 'I wanted to get back into the swing of studying,' and 'I'm finding it's a good training in self-discipline.' Such students wanted the course to be challenging, to stretch their capacity and develop their ability.

We have seen then that students' orientations can have a sizeable impact on their learning, and that it is valuable to ask not only how *much* motivation they have, but also *what* it is that motivates them each individually. Since it is our concern to develop guidelines for design, we need to ask what the practical implications are of this insight. Two strategies present themselves. We could design courses in line with students' goals, or we could try to change students' intentions.

On the face of it it would seem an impossible task to affect students' reasons for studying. Yet we found that many of them simply had not thought through their reasons, and only had a few vague ideas. Some of our examples show that the more specific the reasons the clearer their influence on concerns in studying. We found a slight tendency for students with a greater variety of reasons for study to perform better on course assessment than those with only one or two reasons. Therefore we propose that a starting point is simply to help students to become more aware of their own reasons for studying, and particularly to recognize any intrinsic interest which the course content may hold for them. To this end we have produced a leaflet, *Secrets of Success,* for use in counselling or tutorial work. It can be used to lead students through the process of clarifying their reasons for studying and their goals. Wherever possible, goals should be linked up with the actual content of the course, thus generating intrinsic interest.

More fundamentally, knowledge of the qualitative nature of students' motivation will help the trainer to become more sophisticated in learning design. For example, being aware of the influence of intrinsic rather than extrinsic orientation in promoting effective learning should have an impact on marketing policy. Selling points should be designed to encourage Vi interest. The same applies in selection and enrolment procedures. In one company where we conducted our study employees were being encouraged to enrol on the course because: 'You'll need the qualification on your records to protect you from redundancy.' This directly proposes a purely Ve reason for studying which, as we have seen, is not likely to encourage effective learning.

What of the option of designing courses in line with student goals? Is this a possibility for the trainer who is not in the business simply of providing employees with all the educational opportunities they might desire? In-company open learning is a vehicle for meeting company objectives through effective training. Yet effective training depends on effective learning, which as we have seen is associated with Vi orientations. Vi orientations will occur where students consider course content to be relevant to their own perceived training need. If there is a mismatch between training goals and learner goals it is very unlikely that course content will be seen as relevant, and Ve orientations will result. With students' orientations apparently having a profound influence on what they actually learn, trainers cannot afford to ignore them. 'Well-motivated' students are not just those with a lot of motivation, but those whose interests help them to learn effectively.

In accordance with the person-centred model of learning, in looking at students' reasons for studying we have found signs of a link between orientations to learning and learning outcomes. We have been able to speculate about students' concerns in learning. However, as yet we cannot claim to have thrown light on the process of effective learning itself. To

PILOT VERSION

SECRETS OF SUCCESS

Everyone has reasons of some kind for the things they do. As you think about taking up Open Learning or actually start on it you'll have lots of ideas about how studying might affect your life.

Some benefits will be very obvious — others may be at the back of your mind somewhere. If you've been thinking quite hard about whether to do some Open Learning then you've probably weighed up the pros and cons carefully already.

BUT DID YOU KNOW THAT YOUR *REASONS* FOR TAKING UP A COURSE CAN INFLUENCE HOW *SUCCESSFUL* YOU ARE ONCE YOU START STUDYING?

Students with a greater VARIETY of reasons for studying tend to do better

Students do better if they're interested in the SUBJECT of the course rather than just a certificate at the end

Use this leaflet — by yourself or with a friend or with a tutor — to help you think about all the benefits you could get from Open Learning.

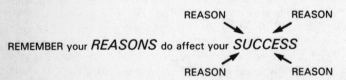

REMEMBER your *REASONS* do affect your *SUCCESS*

Over the page there is a space to write down all your REASONS.
Next you'll find a page of boxes to help you identify the types of reasons you have — and to think about new ones.

Figure 3.1
Secrets of success: an open learning counselling tool.

understand this we must find out not only what students are aiming for but also how they attempt to achieve it. And in our recent study we have been exploring the links between students' orientations, approaches to studying and learning outcomes. As the OU Study Methods Group pointed out (Taylor et al. 1981, p.11): 'Students' orientations to studying are likely to be directly linked to how they approach a particular task.'

How Students approach their Learning

We shall explore the ways in which students approach their learning by looking at the current literature addressing the issue. Ference Marton of Gothenburg University has pioneered an approach that takes the student's perspective. Marton and Säljö (1976) describe how they set a number of university students the task of reading a discursive article and then asked them to explain what they thought the article was about. Clear distinctions were found between the different levels of understanding, and when these were compared with students' descriptions of the way they had approached the article a correspondence was found. Some students took what Marton called a 'surface' approach to learning, an approach characterized by the statement: 'I just concentrated on trying to remember as much as possible.' Those students tended to pick up a few facts but did not fully understand the author's argument. In contrast, other students took a 'deep' approach characterized by the statement: 'I tried to look for the principal ideas.' The students gained a good understanding of the article in question and of the author's argument.

Marton's approach has proved fruitful in elucidating the process of learning in many different studies. His original work used an experimental learning situation, but a number of other studies have looked at learning in its natural setting. For example Diana Laurillard (1979) looked at the way individual students tackled different study tasks. She followed up a number of students through a series of open interviews, and found that they adjusted their approach according to their perceptions of the task in hand.

Others, such as Ramsden and Entwistle at Lancaster (1981) and Biggs in Australia (1978), have incorporated the deep/surface approach dichotomy in inventories of study strategies. Both groups investigated individual differences and found remarkably similar results. By a process of cluster analysis they identified three main dimensions of study strategy which Ramsden and Entwistle label as 'meaning', 'reproducing', and 'strategic' (and more recently (Ramsden 1983) they have identified a further group, 'non-Academic'). The clusters include elements both of students' goals and of their approaches to learning, and thus provide some empirical evidence of how these factors link together. For example, Ramsden's description of the 'meaning' dimension includes both orientation, '*Intrinsic interest in what is being learnt ...*' and approach to study, '*...combined with active attempts to incorporate knowledge and personal experience.*' We can similarly divide his description of the 'reproducing' approach into orientations: '*Concern with qualifications or fear of* *failure...*' and approach to study, '*...combined with a narrow concentration on learning details by rote and following syllabus closely.*'

Although this work does not describe orientations in the same way as Taylor does, it begins to clarify *how* orientations will affect approaches to learning.

We stated our purpose as trying to understand *effective* learning. In pursuing this we have appealed to the work of Ference Marton, who himself refers not to *effective* but to *meaningful* learning, which he defines as: '...a qualitative change in one's way of understanding reality' (Marton 1983, p. 291). We adopt this as our definition of effective learning too. Research has shown that among university students and school children the deep approach leads both to meaningful learning and to academic success (Svensson 1977; Schmeck and Grove 1979; Thomas and Bain 1982). If we are to hypothesize that the deep approach also leads to effective learning at technician level in the Open Tech, it is important that we are clear about the nature of the approach.

What Marton suggests is that learners can be distinguished in terms of their focus of attention in learning. Surface-level processors will 'concentrate on the sign', that is the code, the text itself, and the words and phrases which constitute it (Marton and Säljö 1976). Deep-level processors are much more concerned with the 'message' of the text (Marton and Säljö 1976) or with 'focussing on what the text is about' (Marton 1983). Thus one can express the deep/surface-level processing dichotomy along a single dimension.

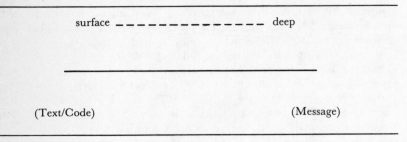

surface — — — — — — — — — — — — deep

(Text/Code)   (Message)

Figure 3.2
The deep/surface dichotomy as a single dimension.

Conceptualizing the surface-deep approaches in this way, we imply that there is a single route to meaningfulness which depends on the student focusing on what the text — or code — is about.

However, meaningful learning does not necessarily depend upon understanding the author's message. Meaningful learning can result from interacting with the text in ways which either go well beyond the author's intention or even by-pass it altogether. For example,

1   A particular text may be written at a superficial level, yet because of our background knowledge we may gain meaning from the text at a level that is way beyond the author's original intention.
2   Alternatively, in reading a text we may find meaning in a way totally unrelated to what the text itself is actually about. For example, Chaucer

didn't write his works in order to convey a message about the use of old English, yet a modern scholar might find his writing meaningful purely for the example of language it provides.

Thus the underlying problem with the single dimension interpretation of Marton's work is that it assumes it is possible to talk about *the* meaning of a text (or task), and that meaningful learning takes place when a student has grasped *the* meaning of the text. This is basically a communication model of learning, not a person-centred model. I would argue that a text — like a painting — has many meanings. The particular meanings that students will gain from a text will depend upon the goals they have been pursuing whilst reading that text. Many goals (particularly in the academic environment) will in fact involve attaining a meaning which the author intended, ie the author's message. However, we would suggest that in pursuing many other goals a learner can attain meaning without necessarily understanding the author's message at all. To avoid confusion we will not use the term 'deep-level processing' to describe this but simply call it 'meaningful learning', a conceptualization of Marton's work which is expressed in Figure 3.3.

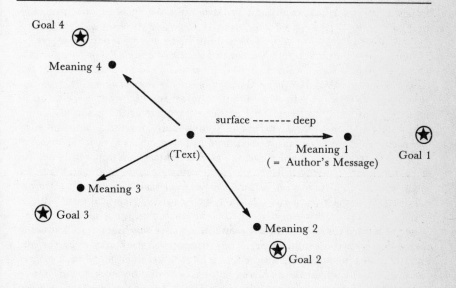

Figure 3.3
The multi-dimensional model.

The model as interpreted in Figure 3.3 is truly person-centred because it puts students' intentions paramount in identifying meaningful learning. The relative view of the meaningfulness of a text also captures more clearly the phenomenological perspective which Marton adopts.

Students' Conceptions of Learning

Where does this lead us as we seek to understand the processes of effective learning? Again the focus is on the role of the learners' intentions in determining effective learning. So we have now followed two routes, one empirical and one theoretical, both of which suggest that effective learning is linked to the nature of learners' goals. Does that mean that so long as training goals and learners' goals are matched up then effective learning will automatically take place?

We set out to explore the links between students' orientations, approaches to study and learning outcomes. Most work on the subject published so far has covered only learners at university level, or school children. In our research we are following Marton's approach but with a very different student population: adult learners studying vocational courses at technician level. We have followed Laurillard's methodology and studied learning in its natural setting, so as to take account of the overall goals and intentions that could influence the study tasks under investigation.

We interviewed twenty-one students from three different Open Tech projects. We wanted to find out from them how they experience the learning process, and to avoid imposing any structures or ideas of our own. We therefore adopted the style of Merton's 'Focussed Interview' (1946). All students were interviewed after they had finished studying a particular section of their course materials. They were asked to describe their experiences of that learning event. Probes were used to explore their orientations to study, the way they had tackled that particular section of the materials and the reasons underlying their approach. Also, in a free-recall situation they were asked to explain a particular topic which had been included in the materials under discussion. Interviews took between an hour and an hour and a half, were tape recorded and have been transcribed in full. The analysis is now underway.

As predicted we are finding that not all individuals with apparently helpful orientations are successful learners. A case study of one of the students we interviewed will provide an example. We shall call him 'Derek'. Derek, although from a farming family, had pursued a career in clerical work until he and his brother (a lawyer) decided to take on the running of their ageing father's farm. Neither of them knew anything about machinery so they had to rely completely on their father's one long-established employee for the maintenance and repair of equipment. Unfortunately neither of the brothers liked this employee, and so as Derek pointed out: 'It's not good for my ego to have to keep running to him.' Therefore Derek decided to enrol on an open learning course in the maintenance and repair of machinery.

Derek's motivation was mainly Vi; he wanted to equip himself to do a job at work. He wasn't bothered about qualifications and there appeared to be no other external pressures on him. In addition there was a strong element of personal involvement and the desire to enhance his independence by developing new skills.

Yet Derek was not a very successful learner, his performance on our learning task was poor, and he had gained well below average marks on a computer-marked test undertaken as part of the course. He was asked about his approaches to learning, and some examples give clues as to why he was not successful: 'I try to remember as much as I can to start off with...,' 'Electrics are a black art to me...,' '...what I'm hoping to do is go over it and if I can remember something different each time...,' 'If I don't understand something more or less straightaway then the best thing is just to carry on ...,' 'I do concentrate, it just doesn't always register...I don't know why...chromosomes or something like that.'

One obvious problem was Derek's lack of confidence. He has labelled himself as a poor learner therefore he does not expect to be able to succeed. Some subjects are simply inaccessible to him, eg 'Electrics', and when he experiences problems in understanding he does not believe that he will be able to solve them and gives up straightaway.

Many of Derek's remarks are consistent with what Marton has described as the surface-level approach to learning. He is trying very hard to memorize as much of the learning materials as possible. Yet such an approach does not match up with the overall aim of being able to maintain and repair machinery. The approach is not so much geared to a goal as to Derek's idea of what learning is all about. There is a hint that he feels that if he can store enough facts about machines in his brain then understanding will automatically follow. The conception of what learning is creates a stumbling block to achieving any goals.

This phenomenon would help explain why study skills courses have often failed to fulfil expectations. It is not enough just to give students the tools of study, ie teach study skills; it is also important to pay attention to their understanding of the task of learning.

Säljö (1979) asked ninety people from as wide a variety of background as possible about their conceptions of learning. Analysing responses to the question, 'What do you actually mean by *learning*?' he developed the hierarchy shown in Figure 3.4.

Conception 1   **Learning as the increase of knowledge**   The main feature of this first category is its vagueness, in the sense that what is given in the answers is merely a set of synonyms for the word learning.

Conception 2   **Learning as memorizing** ... The meaning of learning is to transfer units of information or pieces of knowledge, or what is commonly referred to simply as facts, from an external source, such as a teacher or a book, into the head.

Conception 3   **Learning as the acquisition of facts, procedures, etc. which can be retained and/or utilized in practice**   Compared to the previous conceptions ... some facts, principles, etc. are considered to be practically useful and/or possible to remember for a long period of time, and as a consequence of this they should be learned.

Conception 4   **Learning as the abstraction of meaning**   Compared to the previous two categories the distinctive characteristic of this conception is that the nature of what is learned is changed. Learning is no longer conceived of as an activity of reproducing, but instead as a process of abstracting meaning from what you read and hear ... the reproductive nature of learning is replaced by a conception which emphasizes that learning is a constructive activity. The learning material is not seen as containing ready-made knowledge to be memorized, but rather it provides the raw material or starting-point for learning.

Conception 5 Learning as an interpretative process aimed at the understanding of reality   This conception of learning is very similar to the previous one in the sense that the picture which is supplied in the descriptions concerning the nature of what is learning is very much the same. The reason for making a further distinction is that some subjects emphasize that an essential element of learning is that what you learn should help you interpret the reality in which you live.

Figure 3.4
Students' conceptions of learning (Säljö 1979).

We can see that in effect such conceptions represent a progression from no concept at all, though very simplistic ideas of knowledge as discrete elements to be transferred, to a sophisticated perception of the active construction of meaning. That progression relates very closely to the findings of William Perry, who investigated *The Forms of Intellectual and Ethical Development in the College Years* (1970). Perry's work suggests that conceptions of learning develop through experience of studying. Perhaps the problem for some less effective learners is that their conceptions of learning have not reached a very mature stage of development.

Biggs comes to a similar conclusion when reporting on his recent work in refining his model of student learning (Biggs 1985). Using questionnaire data, he has been able to demonstrate the impact that students' awareness of learning has on their effective choice and use of learning strategy. He suggests that:

> ...if study skills courses...can produce a level of self awareness such that students can perceive what they want and how to get it, and they want it sufficiently, then it is likely that the students concerned could indeed become better learners.

Let us go back to our case study, to Derek and his response to the question: 'What do you actually mean by *learning*?' 'I guess it means remembering what you've just read.' This seems to fit directly into Säljö's level two, a fairly early stage in the development process. We asked all the students the same question during our interviews, at some point after the student had mentioned the word 'learning'. Two-thirds of the responses fell into level three or below. For example: Level 2 — 'Remember that's what it means...remember for the exam.' Level 3 — '...commit to memory the relevant points that need committing to memory, and to be able to use whatever material that I've understood from it.'

But one or two students displayed more sophisticated conceptions of learning: Level 4 — 'I must understand it and know what's really happening and why we've got this final calculation, you know.' Level 5 (arguably) — 'Well, to understand a few more things...I would reason them out from the point of view...well that never even occurred to me sort of thing, because I never bothered to think about it.'

It appears from this brief review that Open Tech students' conceptions of learning might well fit into the same developmental scheme that both Säljö and Perry have outlined. As we analyse our data more fully we will be able to explore the relationship between these conceptions and the way students approach their learning. The evidence suggests that here lies another mismatch, one which creates a barrier to effective learning *within learners themselves*.

Promoting Effective Learning

In our search for the hidden barriers that need to be demolished to make learning truly *open* and *effective* we have attempted to adopt the students' perspective. In doing so a number of issues have come to light.

We have discovered that it is valuable to ask exactly *what* it is that motivates students, and not simply *how much* motivation each one has. The message seems to be that as trainers we must take students' orientations seriously and try to avoid mismatch between training goals and learners' goals. We have suggested a few strategies for this.

The second message is that we need to define *effectiveness* of learning in terms of whether or not the material has become meaningful to the learner. We will be able to recognize such learning by establishing whether or not students have related the material to their own goals. Again, a useful concept appears to be that of match and mismatch. In learning design we should not be concerned to encourage all learners to follow a particular approach. Instead, our priority should be to help learners make their own goals more explicit and enable them to tailor their approach to match those goals.

Finally, we have explored students' conceptions of learning and found that where these do not match with learning goals they form another hidden barrier. It has been suggested that as well as specific study skills training, many learners also need help in raising self-awareness of their own learning process.

The work of the research project forming the basis of this chapter is ongoing. As yet we have only scratched the surface of the insights to be gained by looking at training from the learners' perspective. Perhaps many of the most important barriers still lie undiscovered. Fortunately, practitioners do not have to wait until we have finished our research. They can gain the most by actually using the students' viewpoint to take a fresh look at their *own* training, and discover in themselves the hidden barriers which their own trainees experience.

4

Openness and Learning to Learn

Ian Cunningham

Open learning won't work unless learners learn how to learn (and learning to learn won't work unless there is openness in the learning process).

That sums up my general thesis. Genuine open learning approaches rightly return to learners more control over their own learning. However many such approaches fail because they do not address issues about how people learn (and how they can be assisted to learn more effectively). I want to define and elaborate on the concept of 'learning to learn' and the concept of 'openness' before developing the main themes of this chapter.

The research upon which I have based much of the chapter was conducted at North East London Polytechnic, with undergraduate students in the School for Independent Study and with managers in the Anglian Regional Management Centre. I have also drawn on experience in running in-company management programmes. I have linked the research to particular literature and the key texts are contained in the bibliography at the end of this paper. I have mentioned the relevant names in the text only where it seemed essential to link a particular author with specific ideas.

Openness

I want to define open learning in what to some might seem a very 'open' way. The characteristics of ideal open learning (ideal in terms of my values and my experience of what works) are:

1   It is open to learners to learn
    — when they want (timing, frequency, duration)
    — how they want (modes of learning, for example lecture, seminar, project, meditation, reading or physical exercise)
    — what they want (that is, learners can define what constitutes learning to them)
    All of the above may be constrained by the resources available to the learner and by particular organizational policies. In the case of colleges and universities, learners may need to negotiate what they learn against

the levels or standards indicated for a particular qualification.
2 Learners are involved in assessment of their own learning, specifically in terms of negotiating criteria and methods by which assessment takes place. They are also involved in the process by which judgements are made (for example, on pass/fail, on grades or on marks).
3 It is open to learners to influence the policy and operation of the course or programme. This includes openness in committees and other bodies where key decisions are taken which affect learners.

The three criteria outlined above are met in Self Managed Learning (see Cunningham 1981). A college based course which exemplifies SML is the Post Graduate Diploma in Management (by Self Managed Learning) at North East London Polytechnic (Cunningham, in press). An example of an organizationally based programme is British Airways' Young Professionals Programme (Cunningham 1986).

Learning to Learn

Much of what is written about learning to learn does not even begin to address the issue. If learning is about change (in what we know or what we can do), then learning to learn should be about changing the way we change. I have come to talk about 'meta learning' in order to distinguish my perspective on learning to learn from others. The notion of a meta (second order) process indicates the necessity for us to create a reflexive loop in this kind of work. Applying the notion of 'learning' to itself has to mean something different from just learning more knowledge and skills. So the learning of, say, study skills is just the learning of a set of skills like any other skills. By contrast, the process of learning to learn is not a skill-based activity. It has to be conceptualized in a different way.

My stance is closest to that of Bateson (1972), in his concept of Learning II or Deutero-learning. I will here use a concrete example to illustrate my position. The kind of person who is identified as having learned how to learn may be labelled 'self-motivated' or 'a self-starter' or 'self-confident'. The first thing to notice about each of these terms is the use of 'self' at the beginning. One can argue (see Watzlawick 1984) that such a term can be replaced by an equivalent phrase whereby the word after it is applied to itself. Thus 'self-motivated' becomes 'motivated to be motivated'; 'self-starting' becomes 'starting one's starting'; 'self-confident' becomes 'confident of one's confidence'. We see here again a meta level of operation. Learning to learn is consonant with a range of other second order processes.

I have talked of these as 'second order' processes. The term distinguishes such processes from 'skills', as the latter term is usually used. Skills are associated with things a person can do in a narrow band of human action — skill in driving a car, skill in typing, skill in using a computer, and so on. Such skills are learnable by methods which are well known and well established (for example the use of practice, the giving of feedback, etc.). Learning to be 'self-confident' does not work in the same way. Self-confidence is more appropriately seen as a way of describing the way one does things. One can, for instance, learn the skills of talking in meetings. However there is a recognizable difference between the self-confident performer at meetings, and the person who is nervous and diffident. Essay writing can be identified as a skill. The person who has learned how to learn will feel confident about writing an essay on *any* topic (given enough time to read up on it). Many learners who have learned the skill of essay writing will not do this, believing that they must restrict the application of their skill to subjects which they have been taught. This latter group of learners has not learned how to learn (despite their mastery of so-called 'learning skills').

Issues of Control

Skill based approaches can fail because they are based on the notion of an expert (trainer, tutor, or author) telling learners how to learn. They deny the opportunity to take control of one's own learning, and hence learning to learn processes are sabotaged. If we have access to and can examine the theories about how we learn, we may be able to undermine them. If we can critically analyse theories about our behaviour, and have the freedom to reinterpret them, we are not necessarily bound by them. This allows us to undertake second order meta-level change. As Howard (1971) argues:

> ...a conscious decision maker can always choose to disobey any theory predicting his behaviour. We may say that he can always 'transcend' such a theory. This indeed seems realistic. We suggest that among socio-economic theories, Marxian theory, for example, failed at least partly because certain ruling class members, when they became aware of the theory, saw that it was in their interest to disobey it.

In the process of meta learning the person may need to be aware of how they personally learn, and what alternatives there are to their current learning patterns. They also need the freedom to choose for themselves what they want to learn and how they want to learn.

In Self Managed Learning learners have this freedom thrust upon them. They have to think about how they have learned in the past, and propose learning strategies to be carried out by themselves. They also have to consider the goals and objectives they have, and how well they are meeting these. Participants on a Self Managed Learning course then have to face up to the efficacy or otherwise of their learning strategies, and to learn how to change these strategies if needed. They have to deal with changing the way they change, which is genuine meta learning.

Working with Learners

I want here to take up the role of the tutor/trainer/teacher, and provide a basis for exploring the role in relation to meta learning. To take an example: a learner comes to a tutor with a problem, namely their inability to write an essay on a particular topic. There is a range of responses the tutor might make.

Tutor writes the Essay

This is an option which most would reject. The assumption would be that the learner would not learn much if someone else were to carry out the task for them.

Tutor teaches the Learner about the Subject

This is the commonest mode in education and training. The learner is taught the subject and then expected to be able to write an essay about it. What is apparent is that even within a relatively homogenous group of, say, well qualified undergraduates, there can be a great variation in the ease with which they write an essay and the quality of the work produced.

Tutor teaches the Learner how to address the Problem of Essay Writing

In this approach the tutor is aware that in teaching the subject alone one may not address other problems hindering the learner. The tutor may offer hints and advice on how to get information in order to write an essay and on how to structure an essay. This is the 'study skills' arena, and it has become increasingly popular. The higher educational world has taken up study skills methods and labelled this a 'learning to learn' approach (see Wright 1982).

From earlier comments, it may be apparent that I do not see this as tackling 'learning to learn' issues. Hints and tips about study skills tend to deal with surface issues, and the advice offered does not always address the large differences between individuals. Tips on how to write an essay have, in my experience, been valueless to sufferers of extreme 'writing block' (indeed such tips can make the problem worse, as they imply that there really should not be a problem; hence the blocked person feels even more guilty about their supposed incompetence).

Tutor gives the Learner Instruction on Learning Theory

In the training and management development worlds there has been a growing interest in teaching learners about learning theory as a way for them to learn how to learn (see Mumford 1985). The most widely used theoretical model has been that of the learning cycle, in which the assumption is that learners learn best by reflecting on their experience and developing abstract generalizations from which to try out new behaviours. Hence they generate new experience upon which to reflect. And so on. The most popular model is that devised by Kolb (1974) shown in Figure 4.1. Variations on Kolb include Juch (1983) and Honey and Mumford (1982); more distant relatives include Kelly (1970) and Hampden-Turner (1971). As Boot and Reynolds (1983) have pointed out, the roots of this approach go back much further (certainly to Dewey, for instance).

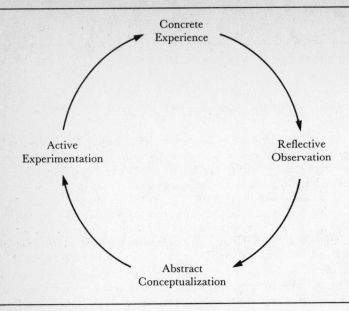

Figure 4.1
Kolb learning cycle.

Learning cycle theory has proved attractive both inside and outside the higher and further education world as it claims to deal very fundamentally with learning to learn. So, for example, courses based on it may advise managers on how to reflect better on their experience, or how to try out new ideas. They may also advise managers on how to put the different learning stages together, with a view to getting them to be the more effective learners.

The problems with the learning cycle theory are threefold. First, as a reaction against theory-based learning, its supporters come to over-value experience, to the extent of arguing, in some cases, that *all* real learning has to come from experience. Hume (1963) from a philosophical standpoint, and Mead (1976) from an anthropological analysis, have both shown how reliance on past experience does not provide a sure basis for future action. Little of what we need to do in the future can be based solely on an analysis of past experience. In fact one of the few things we can be sure about the future is that it is not going to be like the past.

Secondly, I am quite happy to learn a whole lot of things non-experientially. These include the effects of putting your hand in the way of a circular saw, the implications of being shot, the nature of World War I (or any war), the results of catching AIDS — and thousands of other important and useful learnings. These learnings are entirely based on what others tell me and by my own reasoning and I have no intention of ignoring them just because I have no direct experiential reference for them.

Thirdly, research evidence does not support learning cycle theory. James (1980), for example, found that managers did not conform to it (specifically in her research she tested Kolb's model). As she pointed out, one likely reason is that 'additional variables are needed to explain how people gain ability in learning' (p.62). She suggests that her more open research methodology may have produced the more complex picture she found.

In summary, currently taught learning theories do not do justice to what actually happens and can be an inadequate guide to the learner.

Tutor counsels the Learner (or directs the Learner to a Counsellor)

In this option the tutor may feel that the learner is suffering from some personal or emotional problem which is hindering learning. The learner may allude to difficulties with parents or spouse, for instance, as a reason for not writing essays. There are a number of different counselling approaches, the most common being variants on Rogerian, so-called 'non-directive', counselling whereby the tutor/counsellor allows people to explore their own problems, but eschews direct advice. This is a distinctively different kind of response from the four other options so far mentioned.

Among the concerns I have about this approach are, first, the separation of emotional issues from learning issues (to the extent that the tutor often refers the learner to a counsellor, emphasizing the belief in two separate functions). At its simplest this increases costs, if one needs to employ other staff to undertake activities that the tutor feels unable to tackle. More seriously it creates unhelpful schisms, and denies the learner's existence as a whole person.

Secondly, this can be a patch-up-and-mend approach, providing palliatives for learning problems but not fundamental assistance.

Thirdly, from my research (Cunningham 1984) I found that some practitioners have moved away from this approach, feeling that the non-directive style increases turbulence and uncertainty in learners.

Tutor works with the Learner on any 'Patterns' that are not Functional for Them

As with the counselling approach, the tutor will here want to start with the learners and their problems, and not, as in the other four options, start with a predefined solution. The tutor will also wish to adopt a similar mode to the Rogerian counsellor in developing a caring, empathic relationship with the learner. However, there are differences, and they focus specifically around the concept of 'pattern'. In the next section, I shall explore the concept of pattern before returning, in the last part of the chapter, to what the tutor can do in order to work with learners on their patterns.

Pattern

Defining Pattern

If a person continually has problems in writing essays, tutors often label this 'a pattern'. Starting from this commonsense, rather vague use of the term pattern, I want to show that the concept can be made more meaningful and then that it can be used as the basis for assisting meta learning.

O'Hanlon and Wilk (1987) explain the use of the term pattern as follows:

> Sometime during the fourteenth century, the Old French 'patron' meaning 'patron' acquired the secondary sense of 'a model'. It entered late Middle English in the fifteenth century and eventually became 'pattern', a term first used chiefly in dressmaking where it still has the same sense today. Equipped with a pattern or mould or template to serve as a guide, it becomes possible to produce any number of duplicates of an original design. Where we can identify a motif — a distinctive and recurring form, shape or figure in a design, we can speak of the design as being patterned in a particular way. One invariant 'pattern' (in the sense of model) repetitiously applied, creates a recurring pattern. (p.142)

O'Hauton and Wilk go on to say:

> ...whenever we observe pattern in the sense of a 'repeating design' (say on fabric), we can deduce what the pattern or 'model' must have been like from which the design was created through repeated applications of the ('model') pattern. We can ask ourselves, 'What is the smallest pattern which if applied repeatedly would produce this design?' Likewise, in observing human behaviour and experience, whenever we notice — usually from the experience of recurrence or 'here we go again' — that 'there seems to be a pattern here', and seek to identify the pattern, what we are seeking is the model, the mold, the template. And what is this template but the general abstracted from the particular, the general outline or form of what remains consistent or invariant, with all the episodic features or incidental details left out? The search for the pattern is a search for the outline, the general template. It is the search for the regular amidst the irregular, the invariant amidst variation, the unity in diversity. In cybernetic terms, we are looking for the 'constraints' or 'restraints' on variety — the limits within which the variables happen to vary, that which remains the same the more things change. If we can discover these limits on variance — and it is precisely those limits that are invariant — we can intervene to introduce variation going beyond these limits, thereby creating a new pattern. (p.143)

The last sentence here provides the link to what I want to come on to later, namely changing patterns. However, before tackling that I want to add further to the specification of a pattern.

Pattern is not a thing: pattern describes processes, an ordering of events, a sequencing of elements, inter-relationships. To quote O'Hanlon and Wilk again:

As I walk along I can suddenly or gradually change my step, but this only means that at some particular point in time I was walking one way and now at some later point in time I am walking in another way. There is not something in the world called 'my step' which was in the world at both points in time only with something different about it. Likewise I can change my serve in tennis as a result of successful instruction, but this simply means that I typically used to serve that way and now typically serve this way, not that there is some mysterious abstract entity in the world (which I call 'my serve') which somehow has undergone a transformation between then and now. (p.26)

I can elucidate pattern further by reference to five additional concepts.

1   Patterns are *triggered* in some way. A serve at tennis is triggered by the need to start the play, and by the conventions of the game.
2   Patterns are made up of *elements*. In a serve these elements include standing behind the baseline, throwing the ball up, hitting the ball.
3   The elements are to some degree arbitrary punctuations of a *sequence*. A serve is a sequence of various movements by the player over time, and these movements can be broken down into elemental segments.
4   Part of the way in which we make sense of the elements and the sequence is through a process of *mapping*. Thus we can talk of serving using particular coded words (like 'baseline') to link the elements of the serve. We can represent in words what constitutes a serve, and communicate it to others.
5   In a pattern there are *rules* by which the pattern operates. In a game of tennis there are the rules of the game (such as, serve behind the baseline), but in this context I mean by 'rules' something broader. Rules provide the basis by which the elements are sequenced, and they are, in the context of learning, internalized within our own mental frameworks. They include our beliefs and assumptions about the way to do things.

An example of the application of these five concepts is to take the sound pattern we call music. The conductor of the orchestra *triggers* the *sequence* or piece of music in which *elements* or notes are played according to certain *rules* as *mapped* on the sheet music.

Returning now to the example of the learner with a problem in writing an essay, one might identify the following pattern:

Trigger
  — decision to write essay.
Sequencing of elements
  — reading (to gather information)
  — making notes (to sift information)
  — feeling confused
  — giving up trying to write essay.

Mapping
   — the person's mental map might link the notion of an essay with
     interpretations of institutional requirements and with personal criteria
     (for example, the desire for perfection).
Rules
   — essays are difficult
   — essays have to be written in one way
   — confusion is bad and should be avoided.

This dysfunctional pattern is one that is susceptible to change, if one takes
as a focus the person's patterns. I will comment later on methods for changing
patterns. Before doing that I want to say something about the emergent
properties of patterns, and about other ways of thinking about patterns.

Emergent Properties of Patterns

From the description of what constitutes a pattern, there follow some
generalizations. First, there is a *structure* to the pattern as defined by the
sequencing of the elements. This gives a notion of order and form to patterns.

Second, patterns can be conceived of as a process of *relating* elements to one
another. Such inter-relationships can provide the basis for identifying
patterns.

Third, patterns recur, they repeat themselves. That is how we recognize
patterns: they are not one-off sequences. This means that there is an element
of *rigidity* in patterns: they are habitual, and often unconscious.

Fourth, patterns happen over time: they have a finite *duration*. So in
Transactional Analysis there is the notion of 'scripts' which define long cycle
patterns occurring over a period of years, and there are the short cycle
patterns called 'games' which can last for a matter of minutes. Clearly the
frequency of short cycle patterns may be much greater.

Fifth, patterns occur in specific *contexts*. The person having difficulty in
writing essays may have no problems in writing letters. This is because, even
if they were writing about the same topic, the context is different.

Sixth, patterns occur such as to create *linkages* between, say, the person and
the world around them. The tennis player who is serving cannot be considered
as an isolated person. Serving, as a patterned process, is based on the interrelationship of the person, the ball, the racket and the tennis court. The
pattern is not in the person or in the ball or in the racket or in the court; it is in
the linkage of these in the act which we label 'serving'.

The learner reading a textbook can be identified as a system with a pattern.
It is important, though, to consider learner-plus-book, and not either of them
separately. The danger is in the study skills expert offering advice on reading
books as though the reader were left out of the equation. Generalized hints
and tips may be offered to the learner as though the learner's interaction with
the book were ignored. Counsellors can commit the opposite error by working
on the learner's personal problems as though these could be separated out
from the context within which the learner is operating.

Another Perspective on Patterns

So far I have discussed patterns in a very Western mode. The route (root) is from Pythagoras to Bateson (1972) to Neuro-Linguistic Programming (see Bandler and Grinder 1979). The style I have used is relatively analytical. However, there is another way into patterns, and that is through Eastern thought, especially Taoism. The Chinese Taoists have always seen the danger of analysing the cosmos as though '*things*' were the key to its understanding. They instead developed an ecological awareness of great profundity and sophistication, one that Westerners are now fumbling towards. Taoism fostered the holistic perspective on health through the idea of the human body as a pattern of energy, linked to other energy patterns around it. Again this is a view only recently being developed in the West. Capra (1976) has popularized a Taoist patterning interpretation of the sub-atomic world, showing that it is more in keeping with the current evidence from high energy physics than is a model based on an analysis of 'things'.

Despite such developments, most people in the Western world place central importance on 'what something is' rather than 'how it operates'. The learner who expresses 'fear about failing an examination' is assumed, especially by counsellors and therapists, to have a thing inside called 'fear' which needs dealing with. There is no such thing as fear (or any other thingified emotion). People may operate to patterns which induce physiological changes, such as sweating palms, changes in breathing, etc., such that they feel they are afraid. This may indicate that assisting people to change the patterns might remove the unwanted and unpleasant physiological response. But there is no need to assume the existence of 'fear'.

One of the concommitants of the 'thing' view is a belief that meddling with 'fear' and other 'deep seated emotions' should be left to psychotherapists and others 'who know about these things'. If we conceptualize such issues in pattern terms, I believe it is easier to see them as a reasonable and desirable extension of a tutor's work. I do accept, though, that tutors themselves need to develop appropriate patterns in their relationships with learners before they can work in this way.

Changing Patterns

Here I shall explore different ways in which tutors can work with learners on the patterns learners have that are dysfunctional for their learning.

Patterns and Meta Learning

As I said earlier, Self Managed Learning induces learners to address the business of how they learn, and hence come up against the patterns by which they learn. This gives the basis for operating at a meta learning level. The tutor assisting such learners can provide a range of methods for the development of new patterns where current patterns are unhelpful. An obvious method is to talk with learners about their current patterns in order to give them new insights. The example of the essay-writing problem already discussed could be just such a case. However, to provide insight does not necessarily lead to change. The learner may say, 'Well yes I know all that. You've just put some fancy labels on it. But what do I do?' I want to give some examples of what tutors can offer to learners. The following analysis is not exhaustive; the bibliography gives leads to further sources of ideas.

I shall focus the change methods around specific aspects of patterning, taking the five key concepts of triggering, elements, sequences, mapping and rules as starting points. Such distinctions can be quite arbitrary, and the reader could read all of what follows as about pattern change, without making any distinction. But before I look at pattern change in relation to the five key concepts, I want first to address the concept of flexibility in patterning.

Flexibility in Patterning

Generally, flexibility is seen as a 'good thing' in our culture (and its opposite, rigidity, is negatively valued). Most of what we do is done according to rigid patterns, including learning. And when such rigid patterns work there may be no reason to change them. The problem occurs at the meta level: someone who is rigidly rigid has no basis for changing a non-functional pattern. To be flexible about being rigid or flexible is the desirable state. That is, one needs to be in a position to maintain a rigid pattern that works in a particular context, but to change it in a different context. I have a functional rigid pattern for writing papers like this, but when writing a short snappy piece for a newsletter I need to work to a different pattern. I need the flexibility to change across rigid micro-level patterns.

Many learners have problems when they are trapped in a micro pattern which they transfer inappropriately across contexts. People who read novels cover to cover in a linear sequence have problems if they use the same pattern in dealing with text books. The study skills people have much interesting advice to offer on how to read a text book and superficially what I am saying might seem similar. It is not. When I challenge people on their reading style I want to tackle the wider issue of patterning. I am not interested in them just learning to read better; they may learn that, but then continue to throw up dysfunctional rigidities elsewhere. What I want to do is get learners to see the micro pattern as part of a macro pattern, and help them to develop an ability to switch micro patterns when contexts change.

This issue is particularly important when dealing with learners who are in a 'try harder' mode. They have a pattern that does not work, so they try harder to make it work. The crucial intervention is to get them to do something else other than what they have been doing. Unfortunately, many teachers foster the try harder syndrome because they themselves do not have anything useful to offer learners by way of help in dealing with learning problems. A key aspect in developing learning to learn is that of undermining such advice.

Triggers

By changing what triggers off a pattern, one may get a totally new pattern. If, in the essay-writing example, the word 'essay' is a trigger which sets off an unhelpful pattern, then perhaps another word would do something else. If the tutor were to suggest that the learner might write a letter to a friend on the same subject, would this set off a more functional pattern? It is a matter of trying out different words (triggers) to find out which one is most useful.

A related issue is that of anchoring. An anchor, as the term is used technically in Neuro-Linguistic Programming (see Bandler and Grinder 1979), provides a link between an external stimulus and an internal feeling state. So the snake phobic person sees a snake (or even a picture of a snake) and immediately feels scared and anxious. This is an example of a visual stimulus inducing a feeling. However, sound can do the same. A person may hear a piece of music they associate with a happy time in their life and re-create that good feeling as a result.

In learning there are masses of anchors; unfortunately for many adult learners educational settings are negative anchors. As soon as they sit down in a classroom they re-access the bad feelings they had in school. Neutralizing such anchors can be important in liberating a person from a negative pattern that is inhibiting learning.

When running a session I often prefer to set up a pattern whereby the participants and I can enjoy ourselves and discuss ideas in a positive manner. I might begin the session by asking everyone to close their eyes and remember a good group they have worked in. I help them to create a rich re-construction of the past experience, including what they saw and heard. I ask them to open their eyes, look round the room, then close their eyes, go back inside themselves and develop their picture of the 'good group' further, then open their eyes again, look round, etc. I do this about three or four times. Before I begin the exercise I explain what I am doing and why. The aim of the exercise is to associate past positive feelings with the group which the participants are now joining. (When I work this way I like to be explicit about my motives, giving participants the option not to take part.) What the exercise does is to trigger particular patterns in each person which, while unique to them, are set in a positive mode. In this way the whole session usually goes well. (Bandler and Grinder (1979) provide details of the specific techniques by which one can work with anchors.)

Sequencing of Elements

There are a range of methods a tutor can use by which to assist learners in changing the elements of a pattern or changing the sequencing of the elements, or both. One student raised with me the problem that he was so busy taking notes in lectures that he lost the thread of the lecture, a recurring pattern which he found unhelpful and timewasting. I suggested that he went to a lecture and did not take notes but got the notes from a colleague later. This required him *to remove* an element from his present sequence, and it worked up to a point, in that he had to deal with the lecture on a different basis. A more fundamental problem was that he did not approach lectures knowing what he wanted to get from them. His was more of a passive reception of what was offered to him. Tackling this wider pattern involved him to identifying his learning needs for himself so that he could be more evaluative in what he noted down.

An opposite problem was that of a student who day-dreamed in lectures and did not take notes. Getting him to take notes, that is *to add* an element, proved a useful, though not perfect, solution to the problem. Again, the more fundamental aspect of him becoming more discerning about what he went to lectures for was of crucial importance in developing new patterns of learning. As in the first example, changing the old sequence was the first step towards re-patterning. New elements were subsequently needed to create a new pattern.

Other writers have claimed that significant change can be induced just by dealing with the *sequencing* of elements. An example is the following case quoted by O'Hanlon and Wilk (1987):

A man who sought therapy for depression was in a rigid pattern of brooding for hours on end over the impossible situation with his married girlfriend. After extensive questioning, he explained that the way in which his problem got in the way of his daily life was this: he would get this powerful sinking feeling in his chest whenever thoughts of his relationship crossed his mind. If he was with his mother and grandfather at the time he would start snapping at them and being rather nasty. If he was studying, he would abandon his work and go out on a binge of either drinking or spending. As a result, he was failing in his studies, getting into terrible rows with his mother and grandfather, and spending most of the time either broke or loaded or, in his words, 'crawling on the floor'.

We told him that for the next month, as soon as he got that sinking feeling in his chest, he was to write down the time in a little notebook and give himself exactly five minutes from that time to reach a decision. If he was studying he was to decide whether to go on studying in spite of the feeling in his chest, or to go out drinking or spending. If with his relatives, he was to decide whether to be nasty or civil. Otherwise, he was to decide whether to 'crawl on the floor' or to accomplish something useful. He was to write down the decision he reached at this 'choice point'. A month later he reported that he only had to do this once, completing four solid hours of studying after this choice point. He said he stopped snapping at his folks, got on with his studies, stopped bingeing, and said he was 'finding choice points all over the place' and not letting his feelings determine his behaviour. Follow-up indicated that his depression had not recurred. (p.137)

Mapping

One way of thinking about internal patterning is to use the metaphor of a map. We can imagine that people map the world, their ideas about it, their values and beliefs and so on, in some kind of way which is coherent for them. The problem is that people's internal maps sometimes create limitations on their learning. An example was that of a senior manager in a major accountancy firm who had learned (very efficiently) the technical aspects of his work and had learned to be very creative in the way he marketed his firm's services. What he had not done was to learn how to manage his junior staff. He recognized he was not good at it, but seemed to have no idea how to change the situation. His problem was that he compartmentalized his map. He saw that certain areas were ones in which he could be creative, try out new ideas, develop new ways of doing things. As far as staff management went this was in another area of his map, marked 'do as you have always done'. I did not suggest specific ways in which he could change his map: I concentrated on getting him to see how it was possible for him to change his map himself. He then quickly generated options and was able to incorporate the concept of change into the whole of his map.

Changing Maps and Rules

I want here to put these two aspects of patterning, i.e. changing maps and rules, together as some change methods can most appropriately be categorized as working on both. This is especially so in what Watzlawick (1978) has called 'right brain' methods, that is methods which do not operate according to left brain, linear, analytical, reductionist principles. (Watzlawick is clear that the left brain/right brain distinction is not a simple matter of dividing human thinking into two rigidly separate, brain-hemispherically dependent, modes. However, for the sake of this mapping process it remains a valuable distinction.)

Watzlawick discusses the use of chiasm in change, a linguistic form based on a cross-wise transposition of words; hence the root in the Greek 'X'. An example will make it clearer. In talking of the role of a group in open learning, I have used an old chiasm, namely that in the traditional classroom people in a group think together but feel separately whereas in open learning the people in a group need to feel together but think separately. The structure of the switch can be represented as in Figure 4.2.

The concept can assist people to develop an appropriate map and appropriate rules about the use of the group, and to see that bringing learners together in a group does not violate open learning principles (such as personal choice in what one learns). Watzlawick argues that linguistic forms such as chiasms are effective because they are taken in through a holistic right brain mode: they can be dealt with as all of a piece rather than in a linear, one-word-at-time mode. Hence such linguistic forms can foster re-mapping in quite fundamental ways.

Another right brain language mode (according to Watzlawick) is metaphor. The metaphors we hold to describe learning can rigidify or liberate (or both). The classic educational metaphor is to consider the person as a bucket to be filled up with knowledge. The problem is that it is a leaking bucket, so one has to have top up courses every so often to keep the bucket filled. The standard

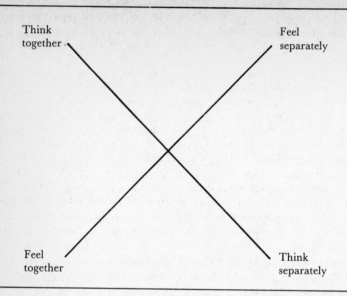

Figure 4.2
Chiasm

training metaphor is about gaps: the trainer identifies existing and desired standards of performance and then trains to fill the gap between the two.

Both metaphors assume a passive role for the learner and hence inhibit learning to learn. An alternative metaphor is of an acorn. Here the idea is that the young person/learner is growing into a mature oak. The acorn has within it all that is needed to produce the oak, provided it is fed and watered. This metaphor assumes that the person has all the resources they need and do not need adding to, or filling up.

At a more micro level, I have often been faced with learners who complain that they are beating their head against a brick wall (in trying to learn something). I suggest that such an activity can lead to brain damage, as brick walls are harder than heads. I tend to go on to accept their perspective that they are dealing with a brick wall (since that is their reality), but to offer alternative ways of dealing with the wall. I might tell the Taoist story of how water copes with walls (flowing round, under, over, through the cracks or whatever) and suggest a more flowing mode of learning. Or I might talk about the supposedly impenetrable Maginot line the French erected before the Second World War to keep out the Germans. And how the Germans dealt with it by simply going round the ends of the line. This kind of work on metaphor may help the person to reconsider their own metaphor, and hence change their learning pattern.

Metaphor change can be seen as part of the more general strategy of *reframing*. The notion here is that one looks at the world (frames it) in a particular way, the frames through which we look at the world are based on our internal maps and rules. Thus if we could look at the world differently this might help us change our maps and rules and therefore how effectively we learn.

As Watzlawick (1978) comments:

...the humorous but by no means trivial definition of the difference between an optimist and a pessimist: the optimist says of a bottle that it is half full; the pessimist sees it as half empty. The same bottle and the same quantity of wine, in other words: the same first-order reality — but two very different world images, creating two very different (second-order) 'realities'. In this changeability of subjective 'realities' lies the power of those therapeutic interventions that have come to be known under the rubric of reframing. Let us remember: we never deal with reality *per se*, but rather with *images* of reality — that is, with interpretations. While the number of potentially possible interpretations is very large, our world image usually permits us to see only one — and this *one* therefore appears to be the only possible, reasonable, and permitted solution, and if we don't succeed at first we try and try again — or, in other words, we resort to the recipe of doing *more of the same*. This is where reframing comes in and is successful if it manages to invest a given situation with a new meaning that is just as appropriate or even more convincing than the one our client has so far attributed to it. That this meaning must be congenial to his world image and communicated to him in the 'language' of this image (is) obvious. (pp. 118/119)

At one level reframing can be about helping learners to see more opportunities for learning than they have done in the past. Hence they change the frame they put around a situation to include the possibility of learning. In working in organizations with managers I have often suggested, when the person has perceived a problem (for example how they deal with others in meetings), that they observe what others do in order to get a better idea of what works and what does not. This reframes events (in this case meetings) to include the option of learning from others.

Confusion and stuckness are marvellous feeling states to reframe (see Bandler 1985; Pirsig 1974). People often say they are confused by something or even that they are stuck and do not know what to do. As both Bandler and Pirsig point out, such a situation calls for new learning. If, as in Pirsig's case, you are stuck with a motor cycle which does not work, you may have to learn something new in order to get unstuck. So stuckness, rather than being a bad thing, is a positive opportunity to learn (and therefore to be welcomed).

Dealing productively with these feeling states requires us to go to a meta level. We have to address the issue of how we feel about how we feel. If we feel all right about being confused or stuck then we can stay with it. If we feel depressed about feeling confused or stuck we may wish to find an easy way out of it. Once again we can see the importance of operating at the meta level in order to learn to learn.

Rule Change

There are some approaches to patterning which may be categorized as mainly to do with rule change. An example was a student on a Self Managed Learning programme who had decided to write up an extensive piece of research she had done. She had a great box full of material but could not face writing it all up. On questioning, I identified what in Transactional Analysis would be called a 'Be Perfect' driver, that is she had a pattern of wishing to produce perfection (and if she could not, of not doing anything). One can classify her situation as having a rule about needing to be perfect in what one writes.

I suggested that I would accept a one page summary of the research, and why didn't she do that (and that I didn't want any more than one page). A week later she sent me an excellent ten page draft article on the research. When we discussed it, she commented that she had felt liberated from having to 'do justice' to the material, and so had been able to write what she wanted. My objective here was to assist her in releasing a pattern and creating a new one. She still has the ability to 'be perfect' if needed, but she now also has the option of being 'less perfect' if needed.

An area that is usually unconscious for learners is the impact of their beliefs and assumptions on how they learn. It may (or may not) be useful to explore such issues with learners. A specific concern for me has been self-fulfilling prophecies.

Self-fulfilling prophecies have usually been seen in a negative light (for example, Rosenthal and Jacobson 1968), and assumptions that learning capacity is limited turn out to be true through their action. However, this can be reversed. I assume that people can learn pretty well what they want. I assume that all students on a course will succeed if they want to. And I act on these assumptions: this is not wishful thinking but incorporated in me as a deep seated belief. So my beliefs come true (almost always).

The crucial step is transferring the belief to others. Learners who have an experience of continual failure do not believe that I believe they can learn. I have to be quite patient, sometimes over a long period, while a person continues to screw things up or wallows in a writing block. Some of the techniques I have indicated in earlier sections may have little or no impact until people start to believe in themselves.

This is quite a fundamental pattern change. It is only possible where there is genuine openness in the learning process, especially in relation to the learner's control of his or her own learning. This returns us, then, to the earlier discussion of Self Managed Learning. The techniques and methods I have outlined need to be seen and used in the context of SML, otherwise they will be misused.

Open Learning and Learning to Learn

It is usually argued that open learning needs learners who are committed, motivated, self-starters. As I suggested earlier these latter characteristics are inextricably linked with the concept of meta learning. A problem arises when tutors/trainers get into unhelpful chicken-and-egg discussions. 'Which comes first?' they say. 'Do we need to teach learners "learning to learn" before letting them loose on open learning programmes?' I think attempts to separate the two concepts are based on the false logic of a cause-effect relationship that does not need to be postulated. In Self Managed Learning programmes learners are working in an open mode and are learning to learn. By virtue of the openness of the learning it is possible to change and develop one's own patterns. If the programme were closed and did not, for example, allow learners to choose what they learned and how they learned, it would deny opportunities for learning to learn. It must be open for the learner to say, 'As a result of trying to write that essay I have realized something new about myself and I want to work on that'. If the response is 'That's not in the syllabus' or 'You're not going to be assessed on that', then such closedness inhibits learning to learn.

Role of Trainer/Teacher/Tutor

Whilst I am against exploitation, I am not against influence. A trainer/teacher cannot not influence. The issue is how we use our influence. Do we attempt to liberate the person so that they can be more self-managing, or do we reinforce dependency? Learning to learn cannot be addressed as an issue without also considering these fundamental factors.

Conclusion

I have tried in this chapter to give a flavour of my perception of learning to learn and the context in which this process needs to be considered. My way of conceptualizing and analysing learning to learn is just my way: I do not propose it as a truth or as an ideal. It is just the best way I know.

I am conscious that I have skimmed over some important points (in order to avoid too much side tracking). However, the appended annotated bibliography may provide a fuller picture for those for whom some of this thinking is new. The literature will give the epistemological and ontological background that I have implied but not dealt with explicitly. These more fundamental factors are an important basis for rethinking perspectives on learning and need to be set alongside the issues I have discussed.

Bibliography

I list here some authors who have been particularly valuable to me in the areas I have covered in this chapter.

Gregory Bateson is the key figure. He has consistently argued for analysing patterns and processes rather than content. The best book is the collection of papers (Bateson 1972).

Paul Watzlawick writes on reframing. He also has pertinent comments to make about metaphor and other patterns (see particularly Watzlawick 1978, 1984; Watzlawick et al. 1974).

Milton H. Erickson exemplified in his hypnotherapy a fundamental grasp of pattern/process issues and of the use of metaphor in change. A comprehensive collection of his papers was edited by Rossi (Rossi 1980).

Richard Bandler and John Grinder have built on the ideas of the above three people, and have taken their notions into practical areas of application. Specific texts mentioned here have been Bandler (1984) and Bandler and Grinder (1979).

The above have also collaborated with Robert Dilts and others in developing notions of representation systems (Dilts et al. 1980).

Bill O'Hanlon and James Wilk are psychotherapists who have been influenced by Erickson and by Neuro Linguistic Programming. Their as yet unpublished book is Shifting Contexts (1987).

There is a great deal written about metaphor, but I think that Lakoff and Johnson's book is the most illuminating (1980).

Chris Argyris has written much useful material on learning and on managerial mapping. A good summary of some of his ideas is to be found in the *Harvard Business Review* (Argyris 1977).

Robert Pirsig is a writer who has linked epistemological and ontological debate to quite practical matters of learning: his classic book is *Zen and the Art of Motor Cycle Maintenance* (Pirsig 1974).

I myself have discussed ideas touched on in this paper more fully elsewhere (Cunningham 1981, 1984, 1986, in press).

I have found John Burgoyne's work valuable, specifically in the way he has developed Bateson's ideas on learning. He and I wrote a paper which elaborates some ideas used in this chapter (Burgoyne and Cunningham 1980).

5

The Challenge of Painful and Unpleasant Emotions

Robin Snell

I shall consider here the extent to which feelings of pain or discomfort during learning are preventable and the extent to which they are an inevitable part of the process of open and distance learning. I shall also consider the possibilities and limitations of strategies other than the 'prevention' of pain, such as 'masking', 'soothing', and 'working with and through' feelings, and the special challenges posed by the open and distance context.

Defining Emotions

Literally speaking, pain is a physical experience and not an emotion as such. Emotions are complex and multifaceted processes, and I think it is a mistake to equate them with biological or physiological states. The point has been made by others, including Macquarrie (1973) and Evison and Horobin (1985). The concept of 'emotional pain', however, suggests that some emotions are rather like experiencing physical pain, in that they are unpleasant experiences which 'hurt', and which at the time we would rather be without. Some emotions are unpleasant without being painful, rather like physical discomfort, and again are feelings that we prefer to avoid.

Macquarrie (1973) warns against regarding emotions as phenomena separate and distinct from thought processes, and Evison and Horobin (1985) suggest that emotions inevitably have 'real time' meanings inseparable from and integral to them.

People probably differ in the way they label or pigeonhole their emotions. The labels I give mine may well differ from the ones you give yours. In recognition of this, I provide some examples below which simply serve to make the point suggested by Berne (1975) that people are likely to draw different meanings from similar predicaments and attach different painful or unpleasant emotions to them. The examples are not drawn from open and distance learning situations, because I want to set a more general context first.

Anguish seems to me to be associated with the discovery that we have been responsible for an accident, an unskilled or clumsy action, or a misjudgement that has had unfortunate consequences. During a group exercise I may make a mistake that only I notice, and feel private anguish because I have let my colleagues down.

Shame seems to be associated with the public exposure of such an error. I may admit my mistake, or it may come to light in a debrief after the exercise. In describing some past experience of mine, by way of contributing to a group discussion, I may suddenly realize, on being questioned by others, that the episode I have described illustrates quite clearly that I acted insensitively, carelessly, etc., and I now feel rather ashamed.

Anxiety and fear, for me, are similar kinds of emotion. In anxiety, I suspect that I am not equipped to deal constructively with something that is unknown or unpredictable, for which I have no ready programme or 'script' to guide my actions. This may happen to me during a somewhat unstructured personal development workshop. Middle managers would, I imagine, have similar feelings during workshops say on 'the skills of interpersonal influence', or similar topics where they are expected to take part in a series of structured exercises. Fear, for me, involves focusing on challenges of a more specific nature, where there is reason to believe that I may not cope well with the situation in prospect. I may fear a visit from a particularly aggressive student whose work I have just failed, either because of an incident in my past when I was attacked or because the student has a reputation for making life difficult.

Suffering for me, is the growing awareness that one has been experiencing psychological damage, impairment, harm or stunting. On a life planning workshop, a participant may come to realize the extent to which he or she has relied overmuch on an over-protective mentor, has specialized too narrowly, or has failed to recognize opportunities in time, all of which may serve to arrest personal development and damage confidence. In addition, the participant may suffer during discussions because of a failure to articulate and explain ideas to the other participants, becoming ever more aware that there is something wrong with his or her skills of communication or self-management in a group context.

Whether a feeling is one of depression or of despair, is, for me, a matter of degree. In despair, I find myself to be a prisoner in an imperfect world, without a hope of realizing my most cherished values, seeing no way forward and no way out. Depression is rather less shattering, felt perhaps by some change agents in organizations, whose best attempts to create a more humane, supportive and purposeful climate of human relations receive continual setbacks or are treated with apathy and cynicism.

For me, all such emotions are painful ones. Other emotions, such as the boredom I feel when unable to find a creative response to a familiar, uninspiring impasse, and the confusion and indignation I feel when people do not act as I expect them to and think they should, are, for me, merely uncomfortable and unpleasant, without being painful.

Because I recognize that the ways I experience my emotions and associate them with particular meanings are special to me, the focus here is on rather a broad range of them, and I will deal in general with the difficulties posed by painful and uncomfortable emotions in the open and distance learning context. Regrettably, space does not permit a critical consideration of the interrelationship between the learning process and emotions that are pleasurable or comfortable.

Emotions and Learning

The connection between a learner's emotional state and the fruitfulness of an intended experience is not a straightforward one. This is the case even with boredom, which on the surface one might judge to be wholly dysfunctional to the learning process.

Boredom

Little has been said in support of boredom as something that may in some circumstances be helpful in a learning context. Colaizzi (1978a) states emphatically that one should not bother learning or pretending to learn anything which one finds boring. Colaizzi's view of learning is that it is a process in which learners build up personal meanings that are of central significance to their lives. Nevertheless, I believe that it is still possible to regard boredom as having a value, since the experience of it may guide someone away from learning in certain areas and thus help them to decide on others.

Marsh (1983) also presents a negative picture of boredom in relation to a learning situation. In her study of boredom on a training course, she reports learners' comments that compartments in the brain were closing off, there was no energy, they wanted things to be different, but did not wish to take responsibility to change what was happening or identify its causes. As she understood the phenomena, other feelings, such as the fear of taking risks, confusion about the role of the two tutors (who also were bored), frustration, and anxiety, appeared to contribute to and be part of an overwhelming and imprisoning atmosphere, which served to block off any learning. She speculates that had the boredom been painful, rather than dull and uncomfortable, it might possibly have had some exploitable value as a spur to action, but in the circumstances it was wholly dysfunctional in that people merely endured it.

The Value of Painful Feelings

Evison and Horobin (1985) hold that 'negative' feelings, those which are subjectively unpleasant such as being anxious, disgusted, cross or gloomy, and which are nasty and possibly painful, focus attention narrowly on the source of distress, impair problem-solving ability and block off all forms of learning except the process of conditioning.

Skemp (1971), discussing emotions in relation to the learning of mathematics, claims that feelings of dislike, bafflement, despair, anxiety or revulsion towards the subject are negative 'patterns' which prevent further learning. He singles out anxiety, in particular, as a major problem, even if it has its roots in early classroom experience and the learner is now an adult trying to learn independently through working with a text. Such feelings, he asserts, are the fault of teachers who have presented material as a set of meaningless rules and procedures insulting learners by requiring them to accommodate their schemata of thoughts to assimilate meaninglessness.

As with boredom, however, the idea that other 'negative' emotions are always dysfunctional to the learning process seems to be an over-simplistic conclusion.

Revans (1979) implies that emotional pain may be experienced on occasion by managers engaged in the process of 'action learning', which he characterizes as a process of development of the self by the self that can involve the manager spending 'more than an occasional afternoon in some Chamber of Horrors that he eventually recognizes as himself'. Revans (1984) argues that the process of developing questioning insight in this manner entails, among other things, 'quandary, query, and qualms', and may involve times of violent opposition, vigorous contradictions and hostility towards fellow learners. Revans also, of course, emphasizes the importance of supportive comradeship among learners. He does not imply that painful or uncomfortable feelings serve a particularly valuable role, but that they are part and parcel of the development process.

Boydell and Pedler (1979) concluded from data shared by participants on a workshop that most significant personal development involved a period of perturbation, crisis, shock or surprise, often accompanied by feelings of embarrassment or fear (although frequently the feelings were more pleasurable). They point out that perturbation does not necessarily lead to developmental outcomes, but that learning resources could concentrate on helping people to learn from it.

Macquarrie (1973) points out that some existential philosophers have regarded feelings such as anguish, anxiety, boredom and nausea as fulfilling an important function in illuminating the grimmer aspects of the human condition and raising questions concerning the meaning of one's life.

Casey (1985) implies that the process of significant new learning entails the turbulent upheaval of deeply-held beliefs, and is marked by feelings of incredulity and fear. He implies that such traumatic change is preferable to periods of stasis where managers may operate in comfort but are imprisoned by unquestioned ways of seeing the world.

Colaizzi (1978b), in trying to illuminate what is involved when significant learning comes from reading a book of one's choice, suggests that the contents point back towards the reader and provide self-illumination that is as likely to be threatening and painful as it is to be consoling. Efforts to uncover personal meaning in this manner are likely to involve effort and struggle even though they will be carried out enthusiastically.

Summary

In drawing together the implications from these various perspectives, I shall distinguish between the processes of learning and of development as Davies and Easterby-Smith do (1984). I regard 'learning' to be a matter of taking on board lessons in the form of knowledge and of tricks of the trade. 'Development', on the other hand, I characterize as the unfolding of individual potential and the building up of mature personal qualities, including an increased competence in the learning process.

Five points emerge from a consideration of the different perspectives so far discussed. First, where the intention is to provide learners with the opportunity for development, it is very likely that they will experience a measure of emotional pain or discomfort resulting from both the new insight they may gain into themselves and the very process of moving from the known and familiar into the unknown. To seek to prevent such pain in such circumstances is tantamount to attempting to block personal development, as the risk of some pain appears to be inherent in learning of this nature, rather like the growing pains some children experience.

Second, where the intention is to provide learners with the chance of developing their understanding of a body of intellectual knowledge or ability to use a set of practical techniques, such as in the field of numeracy, learners may experience painful or uncomfortable feelings arising from memories of insensitive ways in which they have been taught in the past or from the way they are currently being taught. Pain stemming from such sources is dysfunctional and educators are justifiably concerned with ways of preventing it.

Third, whatever it is that the person is learning, some emotional pain or discomfort may arise from the social context within which learning is taking place. Some learners may find their relationships with others to be uncomfortably close. Some may perceive others to be coldly indifferent towards them and feel lonely and anxious as a result. Whilst such discomfort or pain may be a stimulant for personal growth and development, it may also serve to divert attention away from any particular body of knowledge or techniques that the person may be attempting to learn.

Fourth, even if the learners' intention is a narrow one of acquiring an understanding of some body of knowledge or techniques, they may in the process also derive some personal development from becoming more aware of their personal strengths and weaknesses as learners. Although such awareness is valuable, it may be difficult, uncomfortable, or painful to come to terms with.

Fifth, no one advocates the provocation or stimulation of emotional pain or discomfort as a means of promoting learning or personal development. When the intention is to help someone to learn a body of 'content', most concern centres around ways of preventing such feelings, and the extent to which it is feasible to do so. When the intention is to encourage and support the process of personal development, the wider concern is expressed about how to deal with unpleasant feelings.

Strategies for Dealing with Emotions

I have discussed the interrelationship between pain or discomfort and learning or development, as a preamble to a discussion of strategies for dealing with painful or uncomfortable emotions in open and distance learning. The context of 'distance' is one where a programme has been designed to be followed in geographical separation from those with the professional role of supporting or facilitating the learning. Normally, this is also an 'open' context, in the sense that constraints on access to the programme are fewer when attendance requirements are minimal. Ideally, part of this context will include an 'open' philosophy of education which encourages learners to establish their own purposes for learning, and decide on the means through which these purposes are pursued.

I will consider four main strategies for addressing emotional pain or discomfort: prevention, masking, soothing, and working with and through feelings. For each strategy, I will give examples of its actual or potential use, discuss the limitations on its application, and make a subjective assessment of how it may be used to best effect.

Prevention

Those adopting a strategy of 'prevention' will attempt to anticipate what is likely to give rise to pain or discomfort, and try to steer well clear of this in their designs.

Examples

One source of painful emotion that designers of open and distance learning programmes may anticipate is the association in learners' minds between the experience of using the materials and the experience of study in a school classroom, or of doing 'homework'. It is often said that school experience has been for many people emotionally painful. Consequently, attempts may be made to create texts that are as unlike the standard school textbooks as possible. Materials may instead be glossy, contain cartoons, have a journalistic and documentary rather than a didactic style of presentation, and may attempt to tell a story rather than signal the need to engage in rote learning. There may be wide spaces in the margin to write in, but not, importantly, instructions to fill in blank spaces between words. There may be a low word density but not big writing. Any exercises included would not have 'right' answers to look up in the back, any work submitted would not be graded, and any progress report from a tutor that resembled a school report would be avoided.

Designers of interactive video programmes may attempt to prevent the phenomenon of 'getting stuck', with its attendant feelings of self-doubt, frustration and anger, by means of programmes that do not consist of taking learners through a series of loops and gates, but encourage the learners to browse at will through different parts of the programme, cheat as much as they like, and skip bits that are boring.

Similar steps may be taken to prevent impasses with text-based material. It should be possible to design texts that cover quite complex ideas but are conducive to browsing, with a certain degree of skippable redundancy of explanation built into them. A note in an accompanying study guide might advise learners to keep on reading in the event of an apparent impasse, or to skip to the next section if they feel they are going over old ground.

Designers ought to be aware of racism, sexism, and other cultural assumptions within their materials which may cause offence, and which may discount and marginalize groups of the population. Piloting programmes with members of a wide range of minority groups should help to prevent such phenomena, including that of 'tokenism'.

The learner's frustration at wishing to argue a particular point about the materials, but having no means of doing so is preventable by designers inviting and responding to personal correspondence.

Limitations

The limitations on the extent to which emotional pain or discomfort can be prevented stem from the impossibility of predicting and controlling human experience or actions, or of catering for the diversity of ideas and social values. This is illustrated in the following examples.

A designer cannot know precisely what will spark off painful associations with the past for any particular learner. Piloting materials with large numbers of learners may reveal some general trends in adverse reaction, and the materials may be modified accordingly, but to be sensitive to every possible reaction is probably not feasible. Indeed, modifications intended to prevent pain for some types of learner may aggravate the pain of others.

A 'user friendly' computer programme may be designed to prevent learners from making harsh self-assessments, by using kind and soft language to deal with inaccurate responses or illogical decisions. Yet learners reach their own self-assessments in their own ways. My experience of using interactive video as a learner suggests that, however kind and supportive the language on the VDU, if I get the sense that I have been making slow progress I leave the terminal in a rather depressed and subdued mood.

Boot and Reynolds (1984a) have clearly demonstrated that, regardless of the intentions of the designer, exercises intended for personal development give rise to meanings among learners that cannot be predicted and can be emotionally painful and uncomfortable. Engaging with factual or expository material can have similar effects, especially if learners choose to consider questions such as 'What are the implications of understanding this for the work that I do?', and 'What does this tell me about the organizational world in which I have to live?'. Painful conclusions may be reached about the career one has chosen. For example, learners may conclude from working with a package on secretarial procedures that the work of a secretary is characterized by high levels of subservience. A programme on personal practice may portray this, in the eyes of the learners, as unpalatably manipulative. Facing up to such meanings in relation to the work one has based one's career on is likely to set in motion a painful process of self-examination.

Evaluating the Case

Least promising approaches to preventing emotional pain or discomfort involve attempts to predict and control the learner's experience. For example, some designs include branching programmes of such sophistication that every 'reasonable' sequence of learner responses is assumed to be catered for and any potential moments of pain assumed to have been removed. More promising approaches attempt to empower learners to control their own experience. These regard prevention as the prerogative of the learner rather than as a strategy designed in by someone else on the assumption that they can manipulate the learner's experience towards painlessness. A strategy of prevention alone is clearly inadequate to tackle the challenge of painful and uncomfortable emotions in learning, especially where personal development is sought rather than the learning of a body of material.

Masking

'Masking' is an approach which involves attempting to drown out painful emotions by stimulating or amplifying other, more pleasurable emotions.

An Example

The designers of an accountancy programme intended for middle managers without a numerical background may suspect that for many people the whole field of calculations, figures, tables and financial matters is not only dry and unappealing but may also be a source of discomfort and anxiety. They may therefore try to make the course materials aesthetically pleasing, humorous and entertaining. Instead of written case studies, in which the bare financial information is set out alongside questions about possible financial and business strategy decisions, cases may be portrayed on videotape, episodes in which financial information is discussed being interpersed with moments of situational comedy, or even slapstick. The unfolding of events may be presented as a drama; other aspects of the functioning of the business, thought to have curiosity value, may be dwelt on at some length for light relief. The materials themselves may be attractively packaged, folding out neatly and conveniently on the learner's desk.

Limitations

There are inherent difficulties facing those who attempt a strategy of masking, or mixing education with entertainment. This is because people differ not only in their tastes, but also in their reactions to such efforts. Some may conceive learning to be emphatically a serious process, and may be angered by what they see as gratuitious entertainment. Others, having made what for them has been a major step towards tackling something that they fear or have anxieties about, may wonder when the torture is going to start. Given the long build up within the programme, there must be something unpleasant about to happen! At the first sign of any real in-depth treatment of the subject, they may panic, switch off the set, or close the book. There is a risk that attention may wander away from the learning content toward elements of the entertainment, such as the incidental storyline. Even if the content is not simplified, people may feel patronized if they think it is coyly packaged.

Burkhardt et al. (1982) make the point that humour can become tiresome on second reading or hearing. This is a danger whenever education has been mixed with entertainment and learners have to review the material to revise the learning points.

Evaluating the Case

Masking can be attempted in a strong form, almost as a substitute for good entertainment, or in a mild form, a modest attempt to 'cheer up' the learner. Elton et al. (1984) advise designers to confine themselves to cheering up the learner, and for average learners this seems to be sound advice. Perhaps a strong form of masking could be made to work as a way of helping remedial learners to address educational content that they would otherwise find repulsive. As Mitchell (1979) points out, however, research must be done to reveal the effects of borrowing techniques from the world of entertainment and using them in educational programmes. Further research is also needed on whether strong masking (because it may help open up otherwise taboo subject areas) encourages learners to become self-motivated by learning, or whether (because it may make learners dependent upon the seduction of entertainment) it discourages ongoing learning and development.

In mild masking, humour and entertainment can be used to illustrate a serious point or raise issues for reflection (Koestler 1975). The style of some recent journal articles involves linking interesting plots or humorous punchlines with serious perspectives and insights (see, for example, Casey 1985, and Grafton-Small and Linstead 1985). The effectiveness of such attempts does not depend on disguising the content, but rather on bringing out the joy in the learning material. As is implied by Wilson (1980), the temptation to dress learning up as something else stems from a pessimistic view of human 'imprisonment', in the world. It is equally possible to celebrate the learning process as a vehicle for power over one's own existence.

Soothing

What is sought by 'soothing' is the gentle edging out of painful or uncomfortable feelings such as anguish, despair, suffering, anxiety, and boredom, and their replacement by feelings of solace, calmness and relaxation. It is a strategy that some learners choose for themselves, seeking solace from partners or close friends.

Examples

Study guides may include techniques for relaxation among ways of coping with anxiety about or discomfort with the material. 'Soothing' comments may appear in the early part of a main study text, alluding to the need not to worry if the material is difficult to absorb at times, and suggesting frequent breaks from study. They may also be inserted just before the passages which the designers believe to be potentially the most difficult, confronting or threatening.

Computer-based programmes may have a more flexible soothing facility, which does not involve the designer in guessing when the learner may need soothing. They may simply offer, on pressing a Help button, a menu of straightforward, non-educational computer games to choose from, with the intention of allowing the learner to take a break without switching off the machine.

A counsellor trying to soothe, would simply listen sympathetically as learners shared their frustrations, aired their anxiety or complained about boredom. Such a form of counselling support may be thought to offer a facility for catharsis where ill-feelings about the programme are concerned.

Attempts may be made to encourage peer support on an informal basis among networks of learners. During the setting-up phase of a programme, for example, cohorts of distance learners may be brought together for 'community building' exercises, and phone numbers and addresses exchanged.

Limitations

Study guidelines, passages written into the text, or computer facilities designed to soothe may not necessarily be interpreted or felt to be supportive. It is possible, instead, that learners will feel that they are being treated in a patronizing manner.

Whether soothing support is sought from working colleagues and fellow learners, and whether such support is provided sympathetically or provided at all, depends on the climate of working relationships within the organization or the learning group. In some cultures, such as that of the police, where a 'macho' image is still predominant, support may not be sought at all. To seek support could be taken as a sign of weakness and ineptitude, people may not know how to ask for support or how to handle requests or invitations to provide support. Study counsellors may not be visited because of connotations of 'loss of face', or because of doubts about confidentiality.

Evaluating the Case

Experimentation may reveal whether there are any promising approaches to soothing without relying on human contact. If attempts to provide a social soothing facility are to get off the ground at all, then designers and deliverers need to pay special attention to the learning climate of the learner's work organization and/or home setting. If these are not conducive to moments of relaxation or to the expression of feelings, then some other learning centre may need to be created or deliberate and full-scale interventions may need to be made into the culture of the organization. If it can be made to happen, soothing can be helpful. If used on its own without any other strategy, however, it is severely limited in that it makes the learner adjust to the learning task and not the learning task suit the learner's needs.

Working With and Through Feelings

Working with and through emotional pain or discomfort involves using such feelings constructively as a guide to further learning and development.

Examples

I have not yet found any study guides written to help learners to interpret the meaning of their feelings and work out how to act on them. But I think they could include a section setting forth some of the reasons why learners feel bad during study: association with schooldays or other learning situations which were unpleasant; getting stuck because of ambiguous instructions or explanations, or because of 'bugs' in the programme; 'feedback' that is provided in an offensive manner; failure to meet one's own standards of achievement; feeling one's own values are being discounted; coming face to face with conclusions about one's work and one's life that are difficult to come to terms with; or coming across sexism, racism, etc. in the programme. Provided that the range of possibilities is sufficiently comprehensive, it can be suggested that learners identify the reasons that seem to lie at the roots of what is troubling them. Depending on what is identified, there may be a particular piece of advice or information to refer to concerning what to do next. If, for example, learners conclude that they feel bad because of some unpalatable piece of self-discovery, there may be a reference to particular literature available from certain addresses or sources. Literature subsequently sent off for may catalogue self-help groups, organizations which run self-development workshops at a reasonable price, even self-development books or packages which learners may now decide are suitable for the new 'needs' they have identified. If the reason identified is the discounting of one's own values or perspectives, whilst it is unlikely that designers would wish to identify competitors' programmes which might take a different slant, there may be at least an offer of a visit from someone (perhaps the author of a particular part of the programme) to discuss the learner's own views.

It may be possible to build auto-counselling sub-routines into computer-based programmes. These would pose questions about how learners are feeling, about possible ways in which learners may deal with their feelings, and what the consequences might be, etc. There would be a facility to store and print out learner's responses, and suggestions as to how to go about making sense of the input/output, in *preparation* for dialogue with a human counsellor. One would not expect the computer to be a *replacement* for a human being in this context (see Vallee 1984).

A study counsellor may help learners to address emotional 'blocks to learning' (Stuart 1984) that lie at the root of their troubles. For example, learners may complain that they feel idle when 'just sitting with the programme' or feel impatient with having to pick out details from a videotape. In a sympathetic study counselling session, there would be an opportunity to explore whether this was symptomatic of a general reluctance to sit back and reflect, to analyse situations in detail, and to review experience. If this were agreed to be the case, learners then might be advised to persevere with the programme as a means of expanding their range of approaches to learning and developing. Discussions might range into matters of the learner's career aspirations, and possible alternative distance learning programmes may be identified in dialogue. The learners' pain or discomfort may stem from their over-harsh performance standards, and, through counselling, there would be an opportunity to explore issues of 'learning maturity' (Stuart and Holmes 1982) such as whether the learner has had sufficient practice in setting learning goals that are not only challenging but also achievable.

Similar functions to those performed by a counsellor can be attempted by a group of learners meeting together (see Robinson 1981). Possibly they could tackle the programme as a team and address issues of team and personal development and ways of helping one another work through emotions as they go through it (material could be provided to help them do so).

Limitations

Study guidelines and auto-counselling exercises intended to initiate the process of working with and through painful or uncomfortable emotions depend for their success upon the integrity of programme designers and managers. The latter need to be willing to enter, if necessary, into free dialogue (at least by correspondence) with disaffected learners, and to become part of a network of organizations providing services that learners may require. Otherwise, learners may be left with a sense of unfinished business that may add to their initial pain or discomfort. Skilled support from counselling specialists may be limited because of cost, and the effectiveness of counselling from peers depends on their levels of counselling skill.

Evaluating the Case

It seems that the strategies of prevention, masking and soothing all have limitations borne out of the impossibility of predicting or controlling for any one learner where, when and how they will experience pain. Whatever is done, learners are likely to experience emotional pain and discomfort. By necessity therefore, we need seriously to consider ways of helping learners to work with and through feelings. I suggest that designers make it a priority to design and produce study guidelines or auto-counselling exercises that are of maximum possible help to learners in working with, and preparing to work through, emotional pain or discomfort towards constructive action. These facilities should help learners to get more from rare opportunities for peer or professional counselling, and alert them to opportunities beyond the direct scope of the programme. In many organizations it is perhaps over-optimistic to expect peer counselling sessions to be a major resource, unless there is a history of action learning (Revans 1979) or the learners have worked together on an intimate basis before.

Concluding Remarks

What is often achieved without prior contrivance or pre-meditation on residential programmes in addressing painful or uncomfortable feelings is heavily dependent on human relationships and on the facility to catch things as they happen. Designers of open and distance learning programmes who want to provide significant learning are faced with the problem of limited human contact.

Design teams can take positive steps to prevent pain by being sensitive in their writing and programming. A reasonably friendly tone of delivery may serve to mask discomfort. Beyond this, the temptation may be to try over-zealously to affect the learners' emotions, when it is more fruitful to provide materials and set up support systems which learners can use to suit their own particular emotional needs.

Within an open philosophy of learning, one important intention would be to empower learners to address pain in ways which suit them. Learners would be subject to less risk of the pain which comes from being under constraint, and would be left with the risk of the pain inherent in learning.

II
THE APPLICATION
OF
NEW
TECHNOLOGY

COMMENTARY

Both chapters in this section are concerned with the attitude of teachers, diagnosticians and professionals towards the use of new technology in problem solving and in education when that technology threatens their previously indispensible roles. Both John Self and Dent Rhodes leave little doubt that for professional people the prospect of their human presence being replaced by a system of machines and software has limited appeal. And the cooperation of professionals which is vital if delivery systems or learning networks relying on new technology are to get off the ground, will not occur so long as assent implies redundancy.

Both chapters, however, range far beyond the traditional perception of new technology in open learning that is so threatening to teachers: ie an independent learner sitting at a terminal that provides instruction in expert knowledge. Indeed, John Self rules out the possibility of one kind of computer based system, the expert system, being used profitably to instruct novices in a body of specialist expertise. Self argues that no such system would be adequate for the infinity of circumstantial needs and purposes of novices, or match the intricacy and uniqueness of face to face dialogue between knower and novice. The practice of representing knowledge as sets of rules (upon which the design of an expert system relies) may do little justice to the complexity of the knowledge to be worked on.

Self provides an alternative picture of the way in which expert systems may be used, suggesting that a cumulative body of rules in a given subject area may be built up and browsed through by a community of peer specialists and researchers. An example would be a body of educational principles expressed as rules, available on a computer system for consultation by educational researchers who could add to the system their latest findings. Such uses of new technology come close to Dent Rhodes' description of a transactive system: a network of professional peers readily accessible to one another and prepared to share their specialist knowledge with one another via telecommunications and by drawing on computerized data bases and catalogues.

A picture emerges of computer-supported development between and among professional peers, not of the educationally difficult and professionally threatening situation where computers instruct learners. In this way, the learner becomes 'peer' rather than 'pawn'. Dent Rhodes places a corresponding emphasis on control *by* the learner rather than *of* the learner, and on the definition of learning purposes *by* the learner rather than *for* the learner. The idea extends to that of the learner contributing thoughts and ideas through the network for the benefit of other learners.

Despite such possibilities, the question of the extent of openness in computer-aided education remains. Will access to such powerful co-learning networks remain restricted to members of particular professional organizations? Or will they be open to the ordinary home computer user? It is possible that the professionals concerned would find many reasons to prevent such openness, preferring instead to hold on to their expertise.

The conception of professional as 'expert' is particularly justified in some fields: in the pure sciences, for example, or medicine or engineering. There, a decision by the specialists to distance themselves from lay people might be excusable on the grounds that they know more rules which appear to work most of the time. Reluctant to extend access to a transactive network to lay people, the professionals in such fields might prefer to mete out understanding on their own terms, using new technology as a support rather than a replacement for the traditional teacher.

A case for the traditional conception of expertise and dissemination is, however, barely tenable in the social sciences, in management or in the humanities. Many specialists realize that the epistemological paradigms in those fields are built up on a web of ethical and moral presuppositions as well as on conjectures about the nature of reality which are unprovable. The process of teaching is itself such a field of expertise. Attempts to build up an expert system of rules to prescribe good practice, as exemplified by Self, may not be the most fruitful avenue of advance in these areas. A new conception of expertise is needed, perhaps where specialists are respected as advisors on and questioners of strands of argument, ways of seeing and states of the art, but the non-specialist is not treated as a blank-slated novice. Lay people could be regarded as co-inquirers into the social world to which we all belong and which we all play a part in constructing.

Here we return to the transactive system. It would be possible, for example, to build a transactive system around a learning community of 'teaching' staff who see their roles as advisers and questioners and non-specialist learners whose role is one of co-inquiry. Each group could draw on, and be linked to one another through, various telecommunication and computer networks. They might also benefit from meeting together from time to time! If in the social sciences and humanities we can begin to acknowledge the intellectual wealth as well as the frailties of the non-specialist, then we might begin to approach a kind of de-schooled, open, computer-aided society beyond the dreams even of Ivan Illich. If, on the other hand, computer-aided learning networks were to become the sole prerogative of groups of professionals, then a massive underclass of people would run the risk of being confined to exclusion, alienation and isolation.

6

Expert Systems and Computer Tutors

John Self

The learning experience for distance learners will increasingly be provided by the various forms of new information technology. There are two strategies which educational designers may adopt to try to ensure that the experience is effective: they can design a 'package' (such as a video sequence) which, on the basis of their understanding of the learner and how he or she learns, meets the learner's perceived needs; or they can design a system which, on the basis of *its* understanding of the learner and how he or she learns, extemporaneously puts together a suitable activity. This chapter will consider the second option.

The only form of technology which can meaningfully be said 'to understand' is the computer. With appropriate software, a computer can be said 'to be able to follow the meaning of; to have a sympathetic, usually tacit, perception of the character, aims, etc. of; to be expert in; to have knowledge or information of' — all dictionary definitions of 'to understand'. Consequently, for any of the new technologies to be significantly responsive to the learner's needs, a suitably programmed computer is needed. Here I will also assume that the computer is the only medium in use.

A class of computer program, the expert system, has been developed recently which understands a particular kind of knowledge, and is claimed to be invaluable to industry, commerce and even education. The purpose of this chapter is to assess the educational potential of expert systems. I will briefly describe what expert systems are, consider their various possible roles in education, and discuss some of their limitations for educational purposes.

Expert Systems

The word 'expert' in 'expert systems' is *not* an attributive modification; an expert system is not simply a system which is expert at some task (much as its designers may wish that naming it so made it so!); there are many computer systems which are expert but are not 'expert' systems and many expert systems which are not expert. In fact, there is considerable disagreement, even among those working on expert systems, as to a satisfactory definition. This is partly because there is a commercial incentive to call almost anything an expert system. The best that can be attempted at the moment is to list those characteristics which are commonly possessed by systems generally agreed to be expert systems.

The Nature of the Task

Expert systems are designed to perform specific tasks which heretofore have been performed (at great expense, hence the industrial interest) by a small number of human experts. Examples of such tasks are: solving problems about the behaviour of bacterial operons, monitoring the cycle water pollution in a thermal power plant, performing short-term severe convective storm forecasting, and diagnosing negative resist photolithography defects. If you are not one of the small number of human experts able to perform those tasks, you will probably not appreciate their difficulty! But a common feature is that the expert's skills are acquired over many years' experience and not by explicit teaching, since the skills appear to be of the intuitive, informal kind which tend not to be described in textbooks. Not all areas of human expertise are tackled by expert systems. A guideline that has been proposed is that it should be possible for the expert to perform the task reasonably briefly through a telephone conversation — this rules out expertise based on motor or visual skills, among other things.

The Role of the Human Expert

Since the experts' skills have never been formalized, it is necessary for the putative expert system implementer to engage in lengthy discussions with them to try to extract some hypotheses about how the expert tasks may be performed by a computer. The expert system is developed iteratively, with the human experts criticizing and helping to refine successive prototypes. Clearly, the collaboration of the human experts is crucial (although it is not so clear what incentive there is for them to give it). The contrast, then, is with conventional software development where, in principle, once a specification has been agreed implementation proceeds without further assistance.

The Design Methodology

As is suggested above, expert systems are implemented differently from conventional software. With software it is assumed there will be a complete specification of some problem which has to be met by some implementation. If any changes are to be introduced, then (in theory) the specification should be changed and the system re-implemented. With expert systems, we have a style which Sandewaal (1978) describes as 'structured growth'. This has two important implications: firstly, that the system is implemented in such a way that it is relatively easy to understand how it works (or, more importantly, does not work) so that changes and additions can be made quickly and safely; and secondly, that the system is rarely considered finished and never considered perfect — since there is no target specification to meet, refinement of the system continues until and beyond (if one is lucky) the point at which its performance is satisfactory.

The Use of Rule Bases

In order to facilitate this structured growth, most expert system designers adopt a rule-based approach, that is, as each nugget of wisdom is extracted from the experts it is expressed as a rule to be added to those rules previously created. The rules are formal statements of informal knowledge, such as

If the pain is throbbing
and its history is paroxysmal repetitive
and the prodomal syndrome is scintillation scotoma
and there is no concurrent neurological sign during paroxysm
  then the case is probably migraine.

The idea is that each rule should be understandable independently of all the other rules, so that it can be added to the system and subsequently modified, if necessary, without worrying about possible interactions with other rules. The set of such rules is called a production system, for which an interpreter is provided to enable the expert system to reason from the rules to reach some conclusion. In general, the condition parts of a rule (such as 'is the prodomal syndrome scintillation scotoma?') cannot be immediately answered but do occur as the conclusion part of some other rule or rules, and so a chain of inferences is set up.

Plausible Reasoning

The inferences made by an expert system are generally not expected to provide a single 'correct' answer, as conventional software may be designed to do. Uncertainties enter the analysis through the data, the rules and the conclusions they make, as indicated by the 'probably' in the rule above. A variety of techniques, from the formal to the ad hoc, have been designed to enable expert systems to handle such uncertainties (Charniak and McDermott 1985). Some expert systems, for example, use standard statistical techniques such as Bayes' rule, some use formal logical/mathematical systems such as fuzzy logic, and others use special-purpose heuristic techniques.

Introspectability

A distinctive characteristic of expert systems is their ability to examine their own reasoning processes. Whereas conventional software merely provides an answer, expert systems provide an answer plus a justification (if required). This is important because, as mentioned above, an expert system's conclusion is not to be assumed correct, and a user of the system should therefore have some way of assessing its reliability. This is generally done by providing the user with an explanation based on a trace of those rules which the system used to reach its conclusion, a facility which is important during the design stage also, to help the designer and human expert understand how certain conclusions have been reached. Naturally, the explanations should not be in computerese if they are to be understood by users and experts who are not computer specialists. The mind-sized chunks of knowledge expressed as rules provide a convenient framework for such explanations.

The Performance Factor

The bottom line is that expert systems, unlike most artificial intelligence software but like most conventional software, are intended to be profitable. Only a handful, such as R1, which determines the physical layout of VAX computer systems (McDermott 1984) and PROSPECTOR, which advises on mineral explorations (Duda et al. 1978), have been acknowledged financial successes. Vested corporate interests make it difficult to assess the success or otherwise of the scores of expert systems reported in the last few years. Certainly, few have progressed to the stage where they routinely perform in a real environment the task for which they were designed. Even MYCIN (Shortliffe 1976), the best-known expert system, never made it to routine laboratory use, despite the fact that in strict performance terms it was a better diagnostician of bacterial infections than any human expert. Factors other than performance, such as usability and managerial/social considerations, also affect a system's acceptability among its intended users. Medical diagnosis, for example, is a field where decision-makers are legally and ethically responsible for the decisions made, and there is an understandable reluctance to accept a technological innovation without a rigorous demonstration of its capabilities. Since expert systems tend to work on problems without clear-cut correct solutions, the evaluation of their performance is particularly difficult (Hayes-Roth, Waterman and Lenat 1983).

These, then, are the main characteristics of expert systems. They are the product of an attempt to make computationally explicit the kinds of knowledge that human experts have which enable them to perform tasks of industrial and commercial significance. The usual technique is to try to express the knowledge as if-then rules which can be reasoned with and which can form the basis for explanations of the system's performance. Together these characteristics help to explain the present enthusiasm for expert systems in industry and commerce. Let us now consider the possible uses of such systems in education.

Expert Systems in Education

There seem to be three distinct educational roles possible for expert systems — as 'knowledge reservoirs', as the core of tutoring systems, and as a way of expressing educational theories.

Knowledge Reservoirs

If it is possible to take a task like the interpretation of mass spectrograms, which is thought to require expertise and for which no detailed theories already exist, and to implement a computer program to perform that task (as it is in this case — the DENDRAL program (Feigenbaum, Buchanan and Lederberg 1971)), then clearly a body of knowledge sufficient to perform the task has been made explicit enough to be expressible in computational form, perhaps as a production system. There is no reason in principle why this production system should not be considered to be a theory (of how to interpret mass spectograms) and why its creation should not be considered to be a genuine extension of knowledge.

In fact, such a form of theory has considerable advantages over alternative forms, such as mathematical formulae, logical axioms or English prose. It is an *active* form, in that one can actually 'run' the theory to see how it performs, and it is an *explicit* form, in that all the knowledge is up front: it is no more and no less than is in the rules (assuming a standard interpretation of the rules). Indeed, an active form of theory seems the most natural for expressing procedural knowledge, that is, knowledge about how to do something.

Creating a 'knowledge base' is no doubt an educational experience for the designers involved, but once it exists it can be inspected by anyone interested in the knowledge contained. Since the knowledge is that which human experts have difficulty articulating and since the knowledge base may represent the combined efforts of several human experts (and so may be more knowledgeable than any one of them), students may well prefer to consult knowledge bases rather than human experts, who are likely to be scarce and expensive anyway (see, for example, Bundy 1986). The ability of expert systems to provide explanations is essential for this to be effective.

Moralee (1986) describes a similar use of expert systems within a research laboratory, where, as he says, the key asset is knowledge not equipment. The laboratory is experimenting with expert systems as a way of communicating knowledge and keeping it up-to-date. The idea is to provide facilities which enable researchers to browse through what is encapsulated in the system, to get a feel for the issues, to find out what's new, to see how concepts are related: for example by asking questions, such as 'What do you know about copolymers?' (which could be interpreted as 'Show me all the rules about copolymers'). Research and experimentation are obviously needed to clarify the requirements of such a browsing aid. But for a committed researcher it may well be more appropriate than, say, a tutorial on the contents of the knowledge base. Since the flow of knowledge is the lifeblood of a research laboratory, any tool that aids that flow deserves to be investigated.

Tutoring Systems

The most commonly quoted application of expert systems to education is in the design of tutoring systems. The proposal is straightforward: use expert systems which can both perform a task and explain how to perform it as the basis for a tutorial interaction that helps students learn how to perform it too. The proposal is summarized in Figure 6.1.

Clancey (1983) followed this methodology in building GUIDON around the MYCIN expert system. Figure 6.2 gives a short excerpt from a GUIDON interaction.

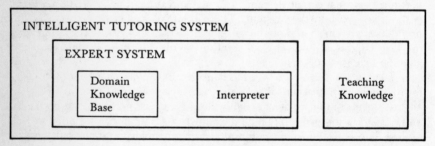

Figure 6.1
Components of an intelligent tutoring system (from Clancey 1984).

FACTORS
The following factors will be useful to determine the type of the infection:

   3a whether the meningitis is partially treated
   3b whether a lumbar puncture has been performed
   3c the duration of the neurological signs
   3d the CSF protein
* 3e whether there are symptoms of Herpes Zoster virus

Factors marked with a * have already been stated. Based on what we have already mentioned, you should be able to conclude about: 3b.

USE 3C
The duration of the neurological signs is 7.2 hours. Using other information available to you now, the duration of the neurological signs enables you to conclude that the type of the infection is bacterial (.2) viral (.2) [RULE 524]

I KNOW 3B
Good. MYCIN has also made a decision. The site of CULTURE-1 is evidence that a lumbar puncture has been performed.

3D
The CSF protein is 40.

HYPOTHESIS VIRAL
You're right, there's strong evidence that the type of infection is viral, given the CSF protein, the duration of neurological signs, and the fact that the patient has symptoms of Herpes Zoster virus. What other facts about this case tell you that the type of infection is viral?

Figure 6.2
Excerpt of GUIDON interaction (from Clancey 1984).

The strategy is to use the expert system's knowledge base to derive an 'expert solution' which, when compared to the student's solution provides a basis for advising the student. The main difference from earlier computer assisted instruction lies in separating the knowledge of the subject from the teaching method, rather than combining them in an unprincipled way. In theory, one should be able to develop tutoring systems for different subjects simply by replacing the knowledge base. Also, as indicated by Figure 6.2, the expert system's ability to evaluate partial solutions and to reason about those solutions allows the tutor to cope with arbitrary student behaviour; for example, to permit the student to collect data in any order he chooses.

Expressing Educational Theories

The tutoring task itself has some of the properties of tasks tackled by expert systems: it is a diagnostic problem (to decide which of several possible teaching actions is appropriate); there is no established theory; the data (such as knowing what the student already knows) is unreliable; and there is a scarcity of expert human tutors (although there is an abundance of average human teachers). In fact, there may be *no* expert tutors, which would of course be something of a stumbling block if one were to attempt to follow the standard procedure to implement an expert tutoring system (ie by long collaboration with a human expert). In any case, the education market may not be sufficiently lucrative to encourage the implementation of expert tutors.

Even so, some recent research could be interpreted as the first steps towards an explicit theory of tutoring potentially expressible as a production system. For example, Collins and Stevens (1982) analysed the strategies of good tutors and tried to express them as a set of rules. One such rule is:

If a student has identified a factor that is relevant to a particular value
and there is a case identified that has a particular value on that factor
  then pick a case that has the same value on the dependent variable, that
  has as different a value as possible on the particular factor, and that has as
  similar values as possible on the other factors.

For example, if Java has been identified as a place that is warm enough to grow rice, then pick a case like Japan which is much cooler but still grows rice.

Fifty-nine such rules are defined by Collins and Stevens and, although they have not been incorporated in an expert tutor, they do demonstrate the kind of theory which could be expressed in the expert system framework.

Other work along similar lines includes Clancey's attempt to manage GUIDON's tutorial dialogue through explicit rules and Burton and Brown's rule-based guidelines for a computer coach (Burton and Brown 1979). Here, for example, is one of Clancey's thirty dialogue rules:

> *If* the factor is not the goal currently being discussed
> *and* there are rules having a bearing on this goal that have succeeded
> *and* there are rules having a bearing on this goal that have failed
> *and* he wants details
> > *then* discuss the goal in a goal-directed mode *and* say that the dialogue is returning to the discussion of the goal currently being discussed.

And here is one of Burton and Brown's twelve principles:

> When illustrating an issue, only use an example (an alternative move) in which the result or outcome of that move is dramatically superior to the move made by the student.

These rules and guidelines are, of course, in need of refinement but that is to be expected in the first stages of expert system design.

Limitations of Expert Systems in Education

While expert systems do hold some promise for aiding learning, they also have their limitations — some of practice, some of theory. At the practical level, most expert systems do not, in fact, adequately provide the desirable features described above (p. 78). For example, the explanatory capabilities of most expert systems are rudimentary and not understandable by a learner. Also, the individual rules often do not make sense in isolation and it is necessary to consider how each fits in with the rest.

These may seem like mere technical problems which further research will soon overcome. But they are a direct result of the implicit theory underlying expert system design. Consider the problem of providing explanations in MYCIN. The MYCIN knowledge base contains the following rules (simplifying greatly):

> *If* he is immunosuppressed
> > *then* he may have leukemia.
> *If* he is a compromised host
> > *then* he may be immunosuppressed.
> *If* he has meningitis or leukemia
> > *then* the infection is known, etc.

MYCIN's 'explanation' assumes that these steps make sense to the user:

> Is he a compromised host?
>
> ** WHY (ie why are you asking me this?)

> To help in determining whether he is immunosuppressed, which would help in determining whether he has leukemia, which would help in determining the infection.

Not surprisingly, a learner does not always find such explanations easy to follow. MYCIN can provide explanations only at the specific level of detail determined by the rules — it can neither go down to explain a particular rule in more detail (ie to give reasons for its correctness), nor can it go up to explain its own problem-solving strategies in general terms. The reasoning steps in an expert system are designed to be as shallow as possible while giving the desired performance. A teacher can provide levels of explanation (involving analogies, for example) whch are unknown to MYCIN and other expert systems. Clancey (1984) describes how it proved necessary to develop NEOMYCIN, with a more explicit, psychologically valid model of problem solving, which could be better related to that of a learner.

In using expert systems in education, there is an assumption that the learner's thinking bears some comparison to the expert reasoning performed by the system. In particular, it is often assumed that the learner's knowledge is a subset of the system's knowledge base. This is patently a false assumption — learner's have much wider knowledge than the narrow, specialist expertise embedded in expert systems, and they also have misconceptions about the specialist knowledge itself and how it is to be used. The performance-driven emphasis on expertise, therefore, makes expert systems the wrong place to start when designing computer tutors — they tend to be unable to relate to the more general (and imperfect) knowledge and problem-solving abilities of the average learner. (Also, of course, the existence of an expert system may render its expertise redundant for humans!)

A more promising strategy is to model an 'ideal student' and to try to understand what an actual student is doing in terms of the model. For example, Anderson, Boyle and Reiser (1985) describe a system for tutoring LISP which contains a 325-rule model of an ideal student and a large 'bug catalogue' describing the errors that actual students can make.

The above limitations of expert systems are only relevant to their proposed role as tutor of (expert) knowledge. They do not affect their roles as knowledge reservoir (provided the users are themselves expert) or as a framework for educational theories. Neither of the latter roles seems inherently unsound and both are worth exploring further to see to what extent they can be made to work.

Conclusions

It is unlikely that expert systems will satisfactorily fill the educational role usually suggested for them: that is, as the basis for stand-alone computer tutors which are sufficiently knowledgeable to guide individual students. There is simply no need for expert systems (as the term is currently understood) to relate to the psychological processes of average learners, as is presumably necessary for individual tutoring in most educational settings. More promising educational roles for expert systems are as knowledge reservoirs, that is, as ways of expressing certain kinds of knowledge so that it may be more easily communicated, and as frameworks for developing explicit educational theories.

7

Interactive Video for Open Learning

Dent M. Rhodes

OPEN (adj.): exposed to general view;
                     subject to question;
                     candid, frank;
                     readily accessible;
                     available for use;
                     receptive to new ideas;
                     not hampered by restrictions.

The notion of 'open' learning in professional organizations is examined here through the use of computer assisted interactive video (CAIV). The examination will include an analysis of different conceptions of 'open' and how they are related to CAIV development. I shall recount our non-success in introducing interactive video into a university, and our very slow, but promising, progress in a medical centre setting. The two organizations themselves are not world-renowned nor even well known outside midwestern America, but I believe they are representative of their type. One significant factor in the analysis is 'time' and its relative importance in the two organizations. Another is the context for instructional technology in professional organizations where decisions are made by nearly autonomous individuals, in this case academics and physicians.

We have also found that one of the problems with interactive video for professionals is their view that CAIV is not conducive to open learning as they conceive of it. I shall describe some innovations in design which we are undertaking to resolve that problem. Given the national variations in video and computer standards, however, I will not venture any predictions as to when we can demonstrate those innovations.

The academic organization in which I do research and development with interactive video is Illinois State University, a former normal school and teachers college that is now a multifunctional institution of some 20,000 students. The university emphasizes undergraduate programmes in the arts and sciences, business, and education. It is one of the largest producers of certified teachers in the country, and all university departments are involved with teacher preparation. Illinois State offers graduate degrees, including a limited number of doctorates, but does not have associated schools of law, medicine, or engineering. The university takes pride in its reputation, justified or not, as a 'teaching' institution.

As a member of faculty at Illinois State University, I believe computer assisted interactive video, like any other means of instruction in a university community, should be 'open' in the sense 'exposed to general view.' My colleague Ms Janet White Azbell and I have no official positions with respect to instructional technology, nor are our academic careers dependent upon its adoption by anyone in the university. We are both members of a Department of Curriculum and Instruction and have an interest in the research and development aspects of CAIV. For about two years we have demonstrated to all and sundry what we and my students have done with courseware development. We have given demonstrations for anyone who may want to see what we do, from the university president to undergraduates in teacher preparation programmes.

We try to be open and candid about the strengths and weaknesses of instructional technology, and give a realistic picture of what it can and cannot do, at least at this point in time. Our approach leaves us vulnerable to criticism from traditional academics who think we have sold out to technology, and from technologists who think we can't possibly know enough to make the machines work the way they are meant to. If our jobs were dependent upon the introduction of CAIV into the university organization, I'm certain we would have joined the ranks of the unemployed some time ago. Academics at Illinois State have as yet shown virtually no interest in developing and using interactive video as a research or instructional tool.

With a well-thought-out marketing campaign, we no doubt could convince some academics that an investment in interactive video would be well worth the effort. Instructional and staff development grants for retraining in the latest technology would help as well. But we are suspicious that these tactics would eventually leave CAIV in much the same category as the closed circuit TV monitors that sit silently in classrooms across the university, or the empty carrels of the computer managed, individualized access, slide/tape/video 'Pyramid' system, whose abandoned control room in the sub-basement of the Education building we have inherited for our work.

Though our colleagues appear to be as open to new ideas as any, they apparently do not believe that open learning through the medium of computer assisted interactive video has any advantages for them. Many academics do of course realize that a learning system which is 'open' in the sense of readily accessible at any time, is self-paced in design and is 'user-friendly' can be quite valuable to students. But, if their actions are any guide, academics at Illinois State do not see that such a system is particularly valuable for them. As professionals in a university organization, academics can make nearly all the decisions which govern their work. Methods of instruction can be imposed only with great difficulty, and the results are seldom worth the effort. Academics can ignore CAIV if they choose, and thus far they have chosen to do so. The door is not yet open for interactive video.

To encourage consideration of the medium, I have suggested, not altogether facetiously, that for some academics CAIV should be the answer to long-standing prayers, in that it would free them from many of the demands of teaching and thus provide more time for research. CAIV can be a labour and time-saving device of some magnitude, particularly when courseware can be developed by design teams in which the research-minded academic need participate only on a limited basis. As one born in the USA, I think that time is important; after all, each of us has only a finite amount of it. But the time factor does not have much appeal in our university organization, especially not among colleagues who are disinclined to do research.

It is my observation that our academics often use instructional media, particularly video and film, to fill time, not to save time for use in other instructional activities. This practice is no doubt related to the administrative norm in the United States of scheduling instructional time in one-hour blocks which must be taken up in some manner. Since CAIV doesn't help to fill 'class time', and indeed could possibly substitute for what an instructor does during class time, one can understand why it may lack appeal. Even if instructors would use CAIV to develop more efficient and appealing course work, they would still need to justify why they weren't 'meeting classes' in the conventional way.

Though my colleagues generally complain that they don't really have the time for the research and quality teaching they desire to do, CAIV does not provide the solution they want. It would be fine for students to have access to an open learning system, but professionally it is not worth the academics developing one. Their time is to be spent doing something more professionally rewarding, whatever that might be. And of course the students' time is not particularly valuable, for as every academic knows, students waste enormous quantities of it.

Our conclusion is that while CAIV as a medium of instruction would have advantages for students, features of our university organization have apparently combined to make the medium unappealing to our academic colleagues. Time constraints, instructional conventions, and the reward system all militate against their developing and using computer aided interactive video.

We have therefore turned our attention to the possibilities of using interactive video in another organization, the Methodist Medical Center of Illinois, located in Peoria, Illinois. The city of Peoria may be noted as the epitome of rock-ribbed midwestern American conservatism ('Will it play in Peoria?' is the question politicians ask), but the Medical Center has a reputation for encouraging innovative practices, especially in continuing medical education (CME) for physicians.

We are concerned with developing an open learning system for physicians at the medical centre, as part of the programme in continuing medical education. Here the physicians become the users, with the content of the continuing education to be provided partially through CAIV. Interactive video will be used to supplement (and for some individuals perhaps replace) the standard series of lectures and tapes now available. Those responsible for continuing medical education have found that few of the taped lectures of visiting specialists or of the commercially produced video tapes are often used. The current situation is neither time nor cost efficient from their perspective.

In our free enterprise, unsocialized medical system, while time is not always equated with money, physicians are acutely aware of the time pressures under which they work. They do not like to spend it unprofitably, whether their goal is more time for patient care, consultation, staying current with the latest research, or perhaps a round of golf. And with continuing medical education for physicians mandated by law in the State of Illinois, there is even more concern that time in CME programmes should be 'quality time', as they say.

Our responsibility to the medical organization is to demonstrate that the technology is capable of providing for self-directed open learning: that is, to supply an instructional service that physicians can effectively use when and if they want to use it. Here courseware design must be tailored to optimize (a term borrowed from design engineers) the control physicians have over both interactive courseware content and structure. Physicians believe, nay, know they are the best judges of what and how they should learn, and acceptance of the interactive video technology is predicated on that understanding.

We are therefore concentrating our efforts on 'converting' existing video tapes to an interactive format since they already embody the type of instructional technology with which the physicians are most comfortable. Of necessity, we rely heavily for assistance on physicians at the centre who are concerned with and involved in continuing medical education. Unlike the academic opinion leaders in the university setting, the physicians with whom we are working seem genuinely interested in CAIV. They are willing to supply the content expertise we need in order to make the best use of the lectures, simulations, and demonstrations available in their video tape collection, and they do not hesitate to suggest where we have misread medical mores. We anticipate that only a few physicians will become involved in the design and development process, however, because that can become quite time-consuming.

Though we are in the process of establishing the means for open learning in the medical centre setting, we are still not satisfied with conventional designs for CAIV. One of the most frequent criticisms we have heard from our professional colleagues in academia (and can anticipate from some physicians involved in CME) is that the courseware for interactive video is too limited in design and execution. They claim that CAIV can't provide for truly open learning because it is hampered by restrictions inherent in the technology. There is only so much one can do with a computer and a VCR or disc player they say, and even if there are a lot of 'bells and whistles' CAIV still has to be pretty much in a presentation, question-answer, feedback mode. Such technology is not very open in conception and doesn't even compare favourably with a book in terms of flexibility, transportability and user control.

Much of this criticism is based on contemporary CAIV designs which have a form of interaction we have designated as primarily 'reactive'.[1] Users are to react to a given subject matter in ways which have been predetermined by the courseware designer, usually by answering questions and responding to directions. A reactive design features program-directed branching and program-controlled feedback. Non-conditional or 'linear' branching directs users through a program in a specific sequence, regardless of any particular responses they might make; conditional branching directs users through a program in sequences determined by the responses they make. The conditions which govern branching may be quality of response (eg correct or incorrect), number of responses, time needed to make responses, or some combination of these. With program-controlled feedback, the type (eg informal, affective), the amount, and the occasion for feedback are determined for users by the program. In so far as possible, learning outcomes are specified in advance for all users. An individual user is able to make few, if any decisions within the reactive program format. Reactive designs for CAIV are therefore restrictive and 'closed'.

We have instead operationalized courseware for continuing medical education personnel using 'proactive' and 'coactive' designs. In a proactive design, users (in this case physicians) have extended control of program structure and can choose the sequence in which content will be presented, the pace at which presentations will occur, the type and occasion for feedback, and, in more sophisticated designs, the 'style' of the presentations, such as didactic, interrogative, or dialogic. In a proactive design, users can also have a choice of content topics to be covered, complexity of content, and vocabulary level. The learning outcomes can be expected to vary from user to user. These outcomes are not predetermined for any particular user and are therefore 'open-ended'.[2] Users make most of the instructional decisions within the program format, and proactive designs thus promote less restrictive and more open learning. In coactive designs, as the name implies, users make some decisions about content and structure but are restricted in others; there are both reactive and proactive features.

To provide examples of materials for self-directed open learning by physicians in the medical centre setting, we have now converted five video tapes from the medical library to an interactive format, with a total of nine different programs. Four of the tapes have two versions each in order to illustrate various possibilities for open learning by physicians; the fifth shows how physicians can use CAIV for patient education. The tapes have been selected by physicians for their utility in CME and include lectures by visiting specialists recorded at the centre, a report of findings produced by a research institute, and demonstrations of a new medical instrument and self-examination for cancer.

The designs reflect the organizational requirements of CAIV for physicians: they maximize efficient use of physician time through individualization and user control. This is done through providing extensive option menus, advance organizers, inserted questions, and search indexes, together with judicious removal of extraneous content such as bad jokes. The courseware designs range from relatively simple indexing to considerably more complex designs which incorporate various forms of video.

For example, we have prepared an indexing program which supplies a 32-segment index for a one-hour tape on dysplastic nevi and hereditary melanoma. For another program, we have taken the same disc on dysplastic nevi and integrated it with a medical video disc. In the latter, a physician from the medical centre presents a video-taped introduction to the program describing its relevance as edited for a particular medical speciality. He also narrates on video tape the salient features of related slides called up simultaneously from the video disc. In another instance, a video-taped lecture on toxic shock has been restructured into an interactive problem-centred simulation. Each of the programs provides the physicians with choices of content, pace, and structure for self-directed, open learning.

The programs are designed for performance self-assessment by the physician and for CME credentialling when appropriate. Here again, the emphasis is on proactive design. In one case, the self-assessment is carried out using a video camera controlled by the user through the CAIV system. After viewing sequences from the original video tape, physicians can practice with a recently developed instrument, the fibre sigmoidoscope, and have their practice sessions recorded on tape to be incorporated into the program. They can review their own practice, compare what they are able to do with examples of expert performance by a specialist, then practice and retape until they are satisfied.

While proactive designs can provide for a considerable degree of open learning, they are still limited by the conventional conception of interactive video — computer control of video tape or video disc. Academics have argued that a significant part of educational development is problem definition and analysis, and although conventional interactive video can provide for some 'problem solving,' it is still restrictive: the problems to be solved are defined for the user. I can say, however, that the technology is now available to expand the concept of interactive video in a way which can make it ideal for unrestricted, open learning in professional organizations. I call this type of CAIV 'transactive'.

In a transactive design for open learning through interactive video, users can communicate through and interact with a wide range of media to develop their own problem definitions, analytic procedures, and possible solutions. While transactive design uses video tape and/or disc as primary technologies, it includes a number of features not commonly associated with interactive video: 1) access through telecommunications links to library collections, literature searches, and on-line data bases; 2) access to computerized dictionaries, encyclopedias, and image collections; 3) provision for direct and comparative visual, written and auditory feedback by peers and 'experts' on performance; 4) provision for outlining, word processing and decision-analysis capabilities.

For example, we are now putting together courseware for physicians to practice skills in the diagnosis and treatment of hypertensive emergencies. The physician will be able to manage realistic situations involving severe or complicated hypertension. We are using the CAIV authoring/delivery systems ProCAL and InfoWriter to develop the courseware. These systems allow us to implement our designs without requiring a knowledge of computer programming.

When used with computer/VCR/video disc interface hardware produced by BCD Associates, the systems will enable us to combine computer tutorials on interventions to lower blood pressure with simulated cases of various crises situations recorded on video tape. We are also including photomicrographs of blood for analysis from an image collection on video disc. A video disc can store as many as 100,000 still frame images which may be called up for viewing in a CAIV system. Narration for these still frame video disc images is to be provided by a physician from the medical centre. The narration will be played back on the audio track of the video tape while the image from the disc appears on the monitor.

We will then use Desqview, a 'windowing' or 'shell' program, to integrate our CAIV program with other software tools. Desqview permits users to move back and forth from program to program as the application requires. Physicians will be able to stop the CAIV program, use outlining/word processing software (eg MaxThink or ThinkTank) to record notes on patient histories and possible diagnoses, then move to decision-support software (eg Expert Choice, Decision Aide) which can help them weigh the various factors involved in making a correct judgement about what should be done.

After further analysis of the CAIV simulations, the physicians can use the computer modem (ie telephone link) to access on-line literature retrieval services and data bases for information from current journal articles or data on drug therapies. For instance, MEDLARS contains abstracts of articles in medical fields; TOXLINE has descriptions of toxic drugs and chemicals as well as their antidotes. As part of the CAIV simulation, physicians will be asked to evaluate unfamiliar drug therapies before the time comes to try them on an actual patient. They can compare the results of their evaluations with the evaluations of specialists available through a random-access audio tape recorder under computer control or on video tape.

If physicians need practice on manipulative as well as diagnostic and prescriptive skills, they can have a video camera record what they do for later self-analysis. We are just beginning to work with the compact disc data storage medium (CD-ROM) which will enable physicians to access the entire Physician's Desk Reference on drug therapies as part of transactive CAIV courseware. With this kind of instructional technology available, the potential for self-directed, open learning in medical organizations is virtually unlimited.[3] Such technology may also help to convince even the most sceptical academics that CAIV can have a place in their organization life as well.

From an instructional design standpoint, this may all sound too good to be true, and for the moment it may be. We certainly do not have a working prototype of a transactive design as yet, and can't guarantee it will be completely 'bug-free' when we do. I had hoped to discuss in some detail the telephone communications possibilities for interactive video and thus include here distance as well as open learning. But that is not to be: it is a classic case of reach exceeding grasp. So at present, transactive open learning in organizations through interactive video is an idea whose time has come, but whose realization has not. We will have to be satisfied with proactive and coactive courseware for the present.

I would most like to report that our courseware for open learning through computer assisted interactive video has been implemented, thoroughly tested, and receives high marks from users. If CAIV is to have credibility among professionals, it must be successfully put into practice: potential is not enough. Information about what happens when the materials are used under a variety of conditions is a necessity in order to make any further progress. We have found, however, that a medical centre is nearly as ponderous and slow-moving as a university, and the process of implementation remains to be completed. Still, as we American baseball fans, especially in Chicago, say, 'wait 'till next year.'

Notes

[1] For an extended discussion of interaction in CAIV, see Dent M. Rhodes and Janet White Azbell (1985) Designing interactive video professionally *Training and Development Journal* 39 (12) 31–33.

[2] I am indebted to Louise Drouilhet of Allstate Insurance for this observation.

[3] *ProCAL* is a trademark of VPS, Ltd.; *InfoWriter*, Data Processing Resources; *Desqview*, Quarterdeck Office Systems; *MaxThink*, MaxThink, Inc.; *ThinkTank*, Living Video Text, Inc.; *Expert Choice*, Decision Support Software; *Decision Aide*, Kepner-Tregoe, Inc.; *MEDLARS* and *TOXLINE*, National Library of Medicine.

III
ISSUES
IN
PRACTICE

COMMENTARY

This section arises from various attempts to develop and run distance learning programmes. It enunciates some of the problems and pitfalls that face the providers of distance learning and identifies some of the key issues that they need to confront. It also contains positive and practical suggestions for tackling some of those concerns.

Schwalbe and Aksjøberg in Chapter 11 draw on lengthy experience in the field to make fundamental points. Schwalbe states that the use of expensive media can only be justified if there is a positive effect on student learning and that two-way communication should be seen to be a function additional to any that is served by the course materials.

Both Aksjøberg and Schwalbe acknowledge the importance of the part played by tutors in distance learning and emphasize the need for tutor training if tutors are indeed to be effective and facilitative of learning.

Staff development is expensive, however, and running like a thread through these chapters is the question whether distance education can be commercially as well as educationally successful.

Both Ballard and Graham and Harrower point out that real choices have to be made between what is economically the most viable and what is educationally ideal. They alert us to a key issue requiring deeper examination and analysis.

Mabey clearly feels that for British Telecom's purpose the expensive medium of interactive video can be a cost-effective way of fulfilling specific training needs. However, the kind of training described is essentially related to technical procedures and mechanical skills which senior management wish a large number of the work force to have or to be aware of.

Csath similarly refers to distance education as a means of reaching a large population of learners in order to convey to them particular information and knowledge. She does not doubt the effectiveness of the approach. It is only Schwalbe, however, who is convinced that purely media-based non-contiguous distance teaching can be effective for educational purposes such as self-development and increased self-awareness.

Ballard describes how the Open University has tried to overcome some of the problems preventing distance education from being more effective in promoting self-development and self-awareness. However, she does not fully address the issue of whether the approach they have adopted is in fact the most suitable one for what they are trying to achieve in terms of community education. Instead she explains the tremendous (and impressive) efforts that the Open University has made to dilute some of the potentially negative effects on learning of this kind, and the financial restraints which control it.

The editors do not think that contributors to this section have been sufficiently lateral or radical in their thinking. None of them move very far from a traditional view of distance education, ie one which emphasizes knowledge dissemination. If such programmes as the Open University community education programme are to become more open and developmental we really do need to be unconventional in our thinking. This is the real challenge for open learning, to provide education which is experienced by the individual learner as being developmental and enabling, but which is available to large numbers of people and is economically viable.

8

Infrastructure and Support

Robert F. Graham and Robert P. Harrower

This chapter outlines the context and recent origins of distance and open learning (D/OL) at the University of Strathclyde Business School, describes the D/OL experience during its early developmental and delivery stages, and concludes by specifying three major policy issues affecting the nature of the infrastructure and student support systems.

The University of Strathclyde in Scotland is a small technological university that was created by Royal Charter in 1964. The Strathclyde Business School comprises thirteen departments and research institutes, plus a section responsible for advanced and interdisciplinary programmes. In 1984/85 there was some 160 full-time academic staff and about 1400 undergraduates, 800 postgraduates and 1200 post-experience and short course students.

Strathclyde was the first British university to introduce the Master of Business Administration (MBA) programme. In 1976 the part-time route to the MBA was established and in 1983 the distance learning route (DL) became available. The MBA student by DL is allowed to take up to five years to complete the Foundation and Elective classes which comprise the instructional part of the programme.

Origins of Distance and Open Learning at Strathclyde

Distance and open learning (D/OL) developments have occurred within a specially created DL Unit responsible for the design and development of the School's MBA programme by DL and a Flexible Management Development Programme (FMDP) funded for a three-year period from April 1984 by the Manpower Services Commission through its Open Tech Unit.

In the Autumn of 1981 a business faculty working party was established to report on the organizational and financial implications of a School development in distance education.

In the summer of 1982 a senior member of the School's academic staff was given the task of investigating and later co-ordinating the design and development of DL materials for the degree of Master of Business Administration. The particular programme was chosen because its general management and interdisciplinary nature would provide a suitable testing ground for the introduction of DL. An additional reason was the calculation that there would be a sufficiently large number of applicants to justify the DL materials production costs. This, of course, echoes Otto Peters' (1971) industrial model which emphasizes, among other things, the cost-effectiveness of large numbers of students receiving standardized materials.

Strathclyde was able to draw upon the distance education experience of two major university institutions directly involved in distance education, Deakin University, Australia and Open University, UK the former of which at the time possessed the only other MBA by distance education programme in the world.

Late summer and autumn of 1982 saw agreement by the School's professoriate to begin the creation of DL course materials for the six MBA foundation classes which constitute the core of the MBA programme (Accountancy and Finance, Economics of the Business Environment, Management of Human Resources, Manufacturing Management, Marketing, and Quantitative Methods). These were delivered to the first cohort of DL students on schedule, in October 1983.

The remainder of the MBA programme, a Business Policy foundation class and a menu of some 8–12 Elective classes, will be produced over a period to October 1987 and thereafter a revision and new class development cycle will be established.

FMDP, the other 'half' of the School's DL Unit, was an experiment in the design of open learning study materials. It presently comprises three basic activities:

1   Development of selected management skills in stand-alone open learning modules created out of already existing MBA DL course materials.
2   Diagnosis, development and delivery of a client-specific, student supported, distance learning foundation programme in ship management for senior officers afloat and middle management ashore, a joint project working in collaboration with representatives from Leith Natural College, Heriot-Watt University, and industry advisors from selected shipping companies and professional institutes.
3   An Open Executive Programme (OEP) which acts as a mechanism through which the individual DL courses that form the content of the MBA programme will be made available to individuals and organizations, with or without university tutorial support as desired.

Features of our Experience

The effects of D and OL on the School has been manifold and some of these are noted below.

The Concept of 'Distance Learning'

In the process of identifying and utilizing the techniques of distance education an explicit distinction was made between distance *teaching* and distance *learning* and the new mode of delivery titled 'distance learning' in order to emphasize the student component of the teaching/learning relationship. Students quite unfamiliar with such learning techniques would be assured that a special effort was being made to facilitate their learning through student counselling and academic support.

The 'distance' component, however, has more than a merely spatial reference and many students followed the distance mode for reasons often more to do with self-pacing, timing their studies to suit their family circumstances, or maintaining their occupational continuity.

The Concept of 'Guided Didactic Conversation'

There was also early recognition of the need for learning materials that were more 'user friendly', more like tutorials-in-print than lectures-in-print, more the type of teaching package that we believe would form the basis for effective distance learning. Thus we came to regard our materials as 'guided didactic conversation' and designed them to operate as such (see Holmberg 1985, pp. 26–30).

Cross Fertilization

Full and part-time MBA students were quick to appreciate distance learning materials and demand access to them. Academic staff also began to recognize their utility and were aware how the teaching situation itself could be changed from the one-way communication model of the traditional lecture to a more intensive two-way exchange based on prior exposure to well designed syllabus-specific learning materials.

Abandonment of Flexible Entry/Exit

Flexibility of entry and exit was abandoned not only for reasons of administrative complexity (such as the need to fit DL students into the existing assessment structure of MBA examinations and Board of Examiners) but also because internal academic staff were neither available twelve months of the year nor wished to manage DL students whose support needs would be completely out of kilter with those students following the same subjects on the other two routes.

Consequently, the DL programme was anchored to the academic year with its October entry and June exit. Three years part-time was the preferred completion time, though a full five years (60 months) has been allowed in the university's Regulations governing the MBA by DL route.

Study Groups

One major problem that was not anticipated concerned the establishment of off-campus, self-sustaining, discipline/subject-based study groups. Because Strathclyde's MBA allows subject choice (eg 4 from 6 Foundation classes) and because DL students have been allowed to take these in whatever order they prefer, study groups have only formed in the larger centres of population such as Glasgow and Edinburgh.

Curriculum Development

The time required to review and create DL learning materials and the shelf-life factor threatens the ability of the MBA programme to respond quickly to changes in the external business environment.

Staff Development

The academic staff involved in the authoring and tutoring by DL (some 40–50 out of a School strength of approximately 160) have gone through what is in effect a form of staff development. They were encouraged not only to think much more carefully about the nature of their course content and teaching skills but also about the students, the need to be much more student oriented in the design of their DL teaching materials and DL support.

In addition, many staff who were originally very sceptical about the introduction of 'correspondence education' in university level programmes have experienced something in the nature of a conversion, finding that their own professional concern, and the public nature of DL materials, has produced a keen awareness of the need to review critically their own products (DL material now in use) and a strong desire to upgrade content, instructional design, presentation, and media mix — the problem here being, of course, questions of shelf-life, academic staff time, and course development back-up.

Resource Scarcity

The University of Strathclyde is not a general, but a specialist provider of distance education. Indeed, distance education has been grafted somewhat awkwardly and in haste on to the School's traditional provision of management education.

Consequently, the development of the MBA by DL was managed largely by addition-to-normal loads on those academic staff involved in the authoring of

DL materials. As this is unlikely to change significantly in the near future, the School's evaluation of the DL experience is likely to be more strongly affected by resource than by educational considerations.

Staff Status

A very limited number of support staff experienced in distance education (providing some course team support, instructional design, technical editing, and production scheduling) have been recruited on a limited contract basis which has introduced differences in status between tenured and contract staff within the School.

Issues of Infrastructure and Support

In a very real sense, distance and open learning is still at the experimental stage and decisions are yet to be made as to whether it will become a permanent feature of the School's programmes. As such, therefore, distance education has yet to prove itself.

It would, of course, be naïve to expect that the value of distance education to the School and, ultimately, the university would suddenly become self-evident. Inevitably it will have to prove itself in much more mundane and practical ways, by some acceptable mixture of the educational, economic, social and political benefits that will accrue to both the School, the university and the wider environment.

But already there are three major issues whose resolution will not only require a great deal of thought but might also set the university on paths which could significantly change the nature of its present educational provision and structure:

1   The level of student advice and support to be given to DL undergraduate and post-graduate programmes.
2   An integrated versus a non-integrated provision of internal and external programmes.
3   The establishment of a properly resourced DL design and development infrastructure.

Level of Student Advice and Support

The level of student advice and support has already been provisionally raised within the Business School. Our discussion derived from a report submitted by the Registrar on the form of undergraduate distance education offered by the University of Waterloo, Ontario, Canada. A key issue is to what extent tutorial support should be an essential aspect of our (Strathclyde's) distance learning programme(s).

In Waterloo's Correspondence Programme each undergraduate degree course (equivalent to a full-time 4-month unit with a credit value of 0.5 out of the 15.0 credits required for a degree qualification) consists of twenty lectures (40 minutes) on ten audio-cassettes, notes, visual aids, samples, lists and textbooks. Each course also requires six practical assignments to be completed and assessed. But there are no summer schools, no local tutors, and no regional officers. Some counselling by telephone is encouraged, but no account is taken of students discontinuing and there is no concept of 'wastage', the cost per student or per graduate being only a small fraction of the cost at the UK's Open University.

Distance education may, of course, range along a continuum. One end stresses individual study and individual non-contiguous teaching solely on the basis of the study materials produced for large groups of students (a large-scale 'industrial' model to which Waterloo approximates). The other end may be barely distinguishable from on-campus study, and involve a large and regular element of face-to-face teaching through residential schools, tutor-led study groups, self-help study groups, telephone tutoring, teleconferencing, student tutor audio cassette exchange, interactive video, tutor student correspondence, and pro-active tutor to student relationships (a small-scale 'handicraft' model similar to that of the University of New England in Australia, see Stewart et al. 1983).

The actual proportion of tutorial support included in a programme in part reflects a balance between the arguments of economic (cost-effectiveness), educational philosophy (such as the need for dialogue between teachers and students if education is not to become mere indoctrination) and educational theory (such as the effect of tutorial support on student motivation and performance). It also, in Strathclyde's case, no doubt reflects the example of other models, such as Deakin University and the Open University, on our own DL development. An example of the latter (educational theory) type of argument occurs in a recent paper (Binsted and Hodgson 1984, pp. 52–53) in which in answer to the question of the importance of the tutoring element in open and distance learning in the management field they note:

> In traditional distance learning programmes, such as the OU, *completion rates* have already been viewed as a key variable. Harrington (1977) has related high failure and withdrawal from distance learning programmes to *loneliness*, and Mathieson has clearly suggested that *learner motivation* is what counts in order for students to complete a distance learning programme. Mathieson goes on to state that *tutoring and counselling* are *important motivational components* (Mathieson 1971). (Italics ours)

Binsted and Hodgson (1984) go on to note a number of other variables that also contribute to distance learning success in management education and training: social pressure to complete/succeed (ie where the social price of failure was too high); the duration of individual courses; the use of self-help learner study groups (thus reducing learner loneliness); and learner interest in course content. We suggest also that the nature and mix of the technical media used to carry the course content to the student (print, audio, video and/or computer) will in part also help determine student motivation and performance.

According to Roberts (1984, pp. 60), of the three major theorists of distance education (Otto Peters, Borje Holmberg, and David Stewart) the latter two advocate the necessity for more effective student support systems. For example, in Holmberg's theory of distance education as 'guided didactic conversation' involving student/tutor interaction in real and/or simulated forms, a major hypothesis is that 'the stronger the students' feelings of personal relationships to the supporting organization and of being personally involved with the study matter the stronger the motivation and the more effective the learning.'

The economic aspect requires its own type of evidence and criteria upon which to base a decision. For example, Roberts (1984, p. 53) states:

> Newly enrolled students are very much at risk of dropping out. A high attrition rate in the initial stages of study has been shown to be the case in every study of drop-out known to the author.

He also makes the interesting point (Glatter and Wedell 1971, p. 54) that

> privately owned external study colleges (in UK) can cover their costs only if they can be sure that a sufficiently high proportion of students drop out early in the programme. If too many students drop out at a late stage of the course, or complete the course successfully, the costs of administration servicing and correction will cause a loss to be made on the programme.

The educational philosophy argument will be decided upon more ideological, though no less important grounds. It may be, for example, that Strathclyde unlike Waterloo is unwilling to assume a position where 'no account is taken of students discontinuing' their DL programme. Commenting on Peters' model of distance education, which emphasizes 'industrial' teaching based on technical and pre-fabricated forms of communication (ie employing cost-effective mass production techniques of artificial communication by mechanical means), Roberts (1984, p. 58) notes that, 'As this competition for greater cost-effectiveness continues, there is a very real danger, however, that institutions will forget that they are dealing with people; people who have individual needs and aspirations, and particular interests and preferences. Peters' preoccupation with mass efficiency is almost reminiscent of the human degradation of the industrial revolution, when the interests and needs of the people were subordinated to the interests and needs of the organisation.' But at present the burden of external evidence from educational theory seems to suggest that some level of tutorial support is desirable for our own MBA/DipBA (DL) students.

The level of student guidance and support is a major policy issue not only because of the economic, educational philosophy and educational theory factors involved in the provision of DL programmes but also because of its implications for the way in which such student resources are organized in future. This leads directly on to the second policy issue to be discussed here.

Integrated Versus Non-Integrated Provision

A second issue which must face the School fairly soon is whether it's full-time academic staff should continue to develop, teach and assess the distance learning programme or should divide these tasks between permanent staff and other, non-tenured contract (full or part-time) staff.

Smith (1979, p. 33), for example, notes:

The Australian integrated mode (as practised by the University of New England) has certain cohesiveness and underlying strength that appears to be lacking elsewhere. These qualities are derived namely from the fact that academic staff are responsible for the total teaching/learning process of writing courses, teaching them through a combination of independent study materials and face-to-face tuition and assessing the students by way of assignments and formal examinations.

Smith (1979, p. 33) notes, however:

In almost all other contexts, in Britain, North America and Europe, 'teaching at a distance' is a shared responsibility. Courses are generally written by authors on a contractual basis, teaching in tutorial sessions and grading of assignments is delegated to part-time or adjunct staff recruited for the purpose and assessment often falls between these part-time recruits and the full-time staff of the institution concerned.

He makes the important point about the latter 'non-integrated' mode:

Consequently there is a distinct tendency for the quality of the product to be regarded with suspicion. In other cases where 'open learning' institutions have been set-up to cater exclusively for off-campus students there seems to be a self-consciousness about operating on the periphery of the educational mainstream.

We have already referred above to the first major issue of student support for DL programmes. It had been noted that the present MBA DL programme is already making considerable development, tutorial support and assessment demands on various departments within the School. As a consequence the possibility of hiving off student support to specially recruited staff has already been informally raised.

With the MBA DL programme now in its third year and already having some 200 external students, it is estimated that numbers will continue to rise for two years and then level off (McDonald 1984, p. 6). This alone will almost certainly force a policy decision as to how the School would apportion the various tasks involved in the development, support and assessment of external students. If, in addition, other postgraduate and/or undergraduate programmes were to be transformed into the distance learning mode, then the pressure for such a policy decision would be even greater.

In anticipation of the 'integrated versus non-integrated' issue we would argue that there is a very strong case for setting up an integrated system within the School. It would involve the following sort of arguments:

— DL is a legitimate mode of delivery for many undergraduate and postgraduate programmes; it could also form an important element in post-experience vocational education and training.

— The whole internal and external teaching-learning process is vastly improved through the use of well designed materials as a basis for the conduct of a more interactive and individualized learning process.

— Development, tutorial support and assessment of DL programmes should be undertaken by full-time academic staff as part of their normal teaching responsibilities in order to harmonize the content, teaching and assessment of internal and external programmes.

— Involvement of full-time academic staff in DL programmes will enhance their development, maintenance and review.

Establishing Properly Resourced Distance Learning

A third major issue involves the provision of an adequate design and development support unit to guide and facilitate the creation of MBA DL courses.

As seems inevitable with the introduction of a major new mode of educational delivery, the School's present DL Unit is under-resourced, even in terms of its present limited commitment to complete the transformation of the MBA programme into a DL format.

The original personnel involved in the production of the first (foundation) stage of the MBA transformation were only two who, because of the magnitude of the task, were able only to provide production scheduling, very limited technical editing and some proofreading. Instructional design was more or less totally absent.

During the last eighteen months two external consultants have, on different occasions, strongly recommended the establishment of an adequately resourced infrastructure of course developers to support subject specialist academic staff in the creation of MBA DL course materials.

The first, Paul Northcott (1985) (Chairman of Australia's Deakin University's Distance Education Unit) noted:

There is a serious omission, in my view, in the DL academic and administrative infrastructure to support an expanding series of DL courses. It is disappointing to return after twelve months and see that the DL Unit has not been placed on a firmer and better resourced basis. You will remember that I discussed the importance of a DL infrastructure ... during my last visit in January 1984. Similar serious criticisms have been raised by Rod McDonald in August 1984.

The second, Rod McDonald (1984) (Director, Educational Services and Teaching Resources Unit, Murdoch University, Western Australia) argued:

Many of the proposals in this report assume that, as in any institution engaged in distance learning, there is a team of course developers able to work with staff producing materials of the necessary quality. Yet it appears that there are no course developers specifically attached to the MBA programme, even though much rewriting will be necessary and more electives are planned.

As a result of the almost total absence of a DL course development support system, personnel on the Flexible Management Development Programme found themselves giving substantial aid and assistance to the MBA by DL development during most of 1984, despite the fact that FMDP had been separately established by external funding to pursue a different and distinct mission.

Consequently, the DL Unit's resource inadequacy was partially obscured and its rectification more easily delayed.

The problem of resources will be only marginally eased by the very recent (August 1985) allocation of a single course developer post to the MBA development side of the DL Unit.

A further and more serious consequence, however, is that resource scarcity has meant both the absence of any systematic improvement in the quality of existing and projected MBA DL print materials and a lack of any opportunity to explore the potential of other non-print media.

Thus, a major issue now facing the School concerns the establishment of a properly resourced DL design and development infrastructure in order to complete the present MBA by DL development, revise and enhance our existing product, explore and utilize the potential of other non-print media, and extend DL to other internal university programmes.

Conclusion

The origin, experience and issues arising from the development, maintenance and delivery of distance and open learning at the University of Strathclyde Business School have been discussed.

The issues that have been raised are not, of course, exhaustive. They are, however, major issues of policy and most educational institutions involved in DL development will have to resolve these either implicitly or explicitly. It would seem preferable, however, that such issues should be solved by design rather than by the trial and error that often accompanies the introduction of new technology within organizational structures.

9

Piñata or Pandora's Box

Christopher Mabey

The decision at British Telecom to produce a number of training programmes on interactive video was taken at about the time that the company (BT) was privatized in 1984. The two events are not unconnected. The need for the BT training department to find cost-effective, high-quality means for developing staff is very much part of the company's retaining its competitive edge in the information technology market. Here I shall give a brief review of distance learning in BT and of a number of recently produced interactive video programmes, then step back to consider more carefully the factors that both internally to the organization and further afield contributed to the original decision to explore the use of interactive video for management training. The strategic objectives are analysed and the ensuing implementation plan is traced, while some of the structures are outlined that were set up to facilitate the operational implications. Throughout, and especially in the last section, which highlights some of the key issues raised during production of the programmes, the intention is to crystallize our learning as an organization and perhaps guide future users of interactive video. Our conclusion, at this early stage, is that the medium has immense potential for delivering wide-ranging benefits across the business — much as a piñata yields rewards to those who break it open. However, mismanagement of its introduction and inappropriate use of its instructional capabilities constitute an equally potent recipe for disaster, akin to the opening of Pandora's box.

Distance Learning at British Telecom

BT's use of distance learning media for training purposes is longstanding. Correspondence packages using audio cassettes and workbooks have been produced on a wide range of technical subjects. Via this very portable and flexible scheme comprising twenty-two stand alone modules, BT students can, for instance pursue a BTEC or SCOTVEC Telecommunications certificate. Other courses using books and audio cover electrical and electronic engineering, digital techniques and microelectronics.

The advent of computer managed learning came in 1976 with a

maintenance technician's course on customer telephone apparatus sponsored by the National Development Programme for computer assisted learning. In 1979 the BT Technical College at Stone in Staffordshire began a major evaluation of computer-based training (CBT) for vocational engineering training. This has been followed more recently by trial use of CBT at locations distant from the technical college. Both ventures have proved not only the effectiveness of this training method but also its cost-effectiveness as compared with centrally delivered tuition.

Then, at the start of 1985, the BT Training department made the quantum leap into the field of interactive video. Trainers have been developing and producing an interactive video for pre-launch sales training on a new digital key telephone system. This was the first such project to go live, and has been used primarily to train field sales force grades in London, Birmingham, Manchester and Liverpool.

Three further appreciation level courses aimed at new managers and new entrants to the business have been produced: introducing the Network, Transmission and Marketing. They make use of the range of media interactive video can offer: computer generated text and graphics; moving video sequences, voice-over narratives; and even some specially designed interactive games. Running times are approximately two and a half hours for Marketing, three hours for Transmission and five hours for Network. Each course is accompanied by a student booklet summarizing key teaching points. The courseware runs on the BT interactive video workstation. A further interactive video utilizing similar laser videodisc technology presents an overview of modern technology in telecommunications.

Each of the programmes is authored in microtext for use on a BBC microcomputer; each is being evaluated on a number of levels: to ascertain the effectiveness of the educational impact, the response of students to the new technology and learning environment, and — where possible — the learning transfer to the job.

Why and how did BT decide to take this radical route for training delivery? As Child (1977) describes in his model of organizational performance, a company's strategic objectives are shaped on the one hand by the owners and stakeholders, and on the other hand by information gathered on past performance and on developments in the environment (see Figure 9.1). Certainly in BT, the developing strategy for harnessing distance learning media has been influenced by both external and internal pressures. It is in the light of the strategic objectives that distance learning plans have been formulated. From these plans and influenced by the unique culture and technology of British Telecom in the 1980s, organization structures and activities have been set in motion to facilitate the transition. Such stages of organization performance provide a framework for discussion of the issues arising from the introduction of interactive video into BT. I shall start with the wider context, then move on to plans and finally give some specific examples.

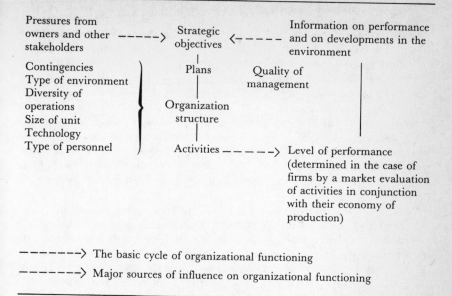

Pressures from owners and other stakeholders $----\!>$ Strategic objectives $<-----$ Information on performance and on developments in the environment

Contingencies
Type of environment
Diversity of
operations
Size of unit
Technology
Type of personnel

Plans   Quality of management

Organization structure

Activities $-----\!>$ Level of performance (determined in the case of firms by a market evaluation of activities in conjunction with their economy of production)

$-------\!>$ The basic cycle of organizational functioning

$-------\!>$ Major sources of influence on organizational functioning

Figure 9.1
Performance in the context of organizational behaviour. (J. Child (1977) *Organisation* Harper & Row Ltd., p. 156. Reproduced by kind permission of the publishers)

The Wider Context

External Factors

At least five factors in the external environment have helped shape BT's strategic objectives. First, there has been a gathering momentum of Government interest and activity in training, with the MSC Open Tech projects and with two interactive videos produced to address the training needs of Job Centre and Inland Revenue staff. Concurrent with and partly stimulated by these government initiatives, the Business Schools have been eager to develop distance learning for management training, with the Open Business School, Henley and Cranfield being among the early producers of high quality material.

A second factor has been the growing number of distance learning initiatives successfully taken by UK industry, with interactive videos being produced on such wide ranging subjects as dealership training (BMW), navigation tuition (Texaco Tankships/UWIST), use of a new telephone system (Jaguar Cars), and cashiering and communication skills (Lloyds Bank).

The launching pad for such ventures was a third factor BT considered, that of technological convergence. Computer based training is well established and has the merit of allowing the student to proceed through courseware in an individual fashion via the branching network. In addition, high quality graphics can be generated by the computer. Video training material on the other hand can have high impact but is passive. Both training media are essentially linear. When both were combined as was done four years ago, first on Umatic videotape and then by Philips' laserdisc, a totally new medium was created greater than the sum of its constituent parts. For the first time, the programme had several potential learning destinations allowing maximum interactivity for the student, and the potential for many different audience uses of the same tape or disc. Moreover, recent progress in the field of authoring has enhanced the accessibility of this medium for programme designers.

The above three factors provide impelling reasons for investigating and experimenting with interactive video but alone they are not sufficient. It would not be unreasonable, for instance, to assume that the dramatic attraction of distance learning — and interactive video in particular — is driven more by flash-in-the-pan technology than the real needs of industrial trainers. However, a fourth and vital external stimulus has been the growing body of evidence concerning the merits of individualized learning for the student, and for the organization.

Cognitive psychologists maintain that beyond puberty the propensity of our brains to assimilate new information decreases markedly. However, new skills or knowledge are more likely to be retained in our long-term memory if they are broken down into bite-sized chunks and repeated several times over a limited period. Retention is ensured when the fresh information is followed up by timely and appropriate feedback (Hudson 1985). In addition, the appropriate and artful synchronization of audio and visual signals characteristic of interactive video helps the brain make sense of ambiguous information and arrive at a relatively accurate and undistorted perception of content material (Wheaton 1984). Furthermore, it is a fairly familiar training axiom that we retain about 25% of what we hear, 45% of what we hear *and* see, and around 70% of what we hear, see and do. In other words the physical activity connected with the learning point is more likely to engage the long-term memory networks. Finally, motivation is enhanced when students are able to study at their own pace and to start with material most relevant to their needs. These various aspects of learning theory together suggest the potency of something like interactive video as an effective learning experience for an individual.

How does the employer benefit? The National Computer Centre cite two studies where subjects trained in an individualized system showed statistically better results than subjects trained in a non-individualized system, and where mastery learning methods increase retention and transfer of learning over conventional approaches (NCC Ltd 1985). Little research has yet been done to compare the effectiveness of Interactive video against conventional instruction, but the findings of controlled experiments published so far look promising. Most promising is the time saved in completely training over those not using interactive videodisc (Kettner and Carr 1983). Other studies, in addition to time saving, also record enhanced performance among interactive video students when measured by a test at the end of the programme and one week later (Bunderson et al, 1981) and by examination seventeen days after the training (Ebner et al 1984). Also encouraging is that virtually all these studies found students reacting favourably to the new delivery techniques.

The reduction in time taken to complete training, together with the lower attrition rate of motivated students can only decrease costs. With well planned training delivery, the materials, facilities and equipment can be in almost constant use, thus minimizing overheads. Meanwhile the substantial travel and accommodation costs inherent in centralized, residential training are avoided.

This brings us to the fifth external factor: the reality of a competitive and rapidly changing business environment. In the train of privatization the responsibility has heightened for the BT Training department to design and produce cost-effective training which meets the needs of the business. If the supply of training courses lags significantly behind demand, the result to BT could be a loss of efficiency and profit.

These were the salient factors of the environment as BT made the transition from nationalized industry to private corporation. No single factor proved the case for substantial expansion of distance learning activity, but when considered together, the threads of governmental, educational, psychological and technological enthusiasm woven into the backcloth of commercial viability impressed on the company the necessity at least to explore the radically new training solutions.

Internal Influences

Pressures from within an organization also play their part in shaping strategy. The demand for training from BT's operational departments is considerable. Most of the 235,000 employees will at some stage require training or re-training in management, financial awareness or technical areas. Much of this training, especially on the engineering side, is in the understanding and maintenance of sophisticated electronic equipment, where real 'hands on' experience is vital but not always practicable. Also the pace of technological change now means that refresher courses and re-training are a regular occurrence for a vast number of functional experts throughout the business. For these reasons computer based training — adept at delivering precise, high quality graphics, diagnostic lessons and computer simulations — has already been harnessed for training purposes, but interactive video also commends itself.

1984/1985 has also seen the restructuring of the Local Communication Services division, constituting 85% of BT employees. This decentralization, with 30 districts outside London replacing the 61 old telephone areas and acting as more autonomous management units, has had an interesting impact on training. More than ever, the emphasis is on the business responding to the customer and being market- rather than product-led. The implication is that training will be more tailored to local needs and will be the responsibility of line managers, who will themselves require training assistance in managing the organizational change.

Thus, the questions facing the Training department were: how to train a high throughput of geographically spread employees most cost-effectively? How to design and deliver training material with a high technical and/or graphic content? How to facilitate retraining with minimum disruption? How to cut down the costs of centralized training that can tie up capital costs? How to support local management in equipping staff for competitive and effective customer service?

Strategic Objectives

It was in response both to developments in the environment and to the internal dynamics of the organization that a training strategy was formulated at BT. On an essentially pragmatic level, it was determined to meet the training need with the most effective and economic means available; to fail in this would simply mean customers within the business looking elsewhere for their training. Thus there was a commitment to harness the most advanced and appropriate technology for the delivery of training.

From this fairly straightforward intent a number of slightly more subtle and far-reaching ramifications flowed, and this is where we encounter our piñata or pandora's box. For those not familiar with the word piñata allow me to recall my eldest daughter's eighth birthday. We were visiting friends on the outskirts of Mexico City and in faithful indigenous style they spent a day or so filling a large clay pot with local goodies (nuts, sweets, fruit and the like), decorating it gaudily until it was utterly camouflaged and finally stringing it up on the washing line. At the party, little guests made earnest efforts with a stick to break open the piñata as it swung above their heads. Little by little it submitted to the beating and disgorged its contents. The preparation had seemed highly elaborate but the delight on the birthday faces more than compensated. Without taking the analogy too far, clear parallels with the implementation of distance learning can be seen, with the highly attractive piñata representing the technological wizardry of a highly interactive training medium which, in fact, is nothing more than a clay jar — a vessel or vehicle — which carries within it all sorts of potential benefits for students, training managers, and the business as a whole. Certainly its introduction requires painstaking preparation, and to be sure its appearance is impressive, but its presence is to enhance the learning experience and the back-at-work learning transfer, and by implication, the performance of the organization. This all assumes that what emerges from the technology is beneficial. There are arguments to suggest that the reverse is true; that indiscriminant dabbling with distance learning can cause more problems than it solves; that, in short, it is tantamount to opening up Pandora's box.

There are at least four ways in which it is likely that the more favourable interpretation will hold for BT. First is the gradual strategic shift in the business away from training which is generalist, predetermined and tutor led to training in which the trainee has greater responsibility for his or her own learning. Second is the emerging role of the Training department in anticipating business training needs and helping to shape the future rather than providing solutions to historical problems. Third and fourth are the ways in which distance learning actually provides the opportunity for the Training department to enhance its professionalism, and build the skills of their tutors and of those line and training managers responsible at a local level. These strands of strategy will be explored in more detail below.

Increasing Learner Responsibility

Akin to many other large bureaucratic organizations, BT has traditionally met its training need by devising syllabus-based courses, often covering several unrelated subject areas in the same course and typically delivered in a central location. In some ways this approach was not appropriate for a paternalistic company, unpestered by direct competition, whose employees were likely to be long-serving and loyal. As discussed earlier, however, each of these characteristics has been contorted drastically over recent years, calling for very different styles of training. For a number of reasons there is now a much higher premium on making the learner, rather than the syllabus, the centre of gravity for training purposes: to start with the issues he or she is facing in the workplace, and to work with this as raw material for action learning, to cultivate the experience of learning as much as the content itself. This is likely to mean greater 'pay-off' back at the job; it will undoubtedly enhance the trainee's motivation and, not unimportantly, it will give the tutor scope for creativity in constructing the learning environment. There is no doubt that this process of change was underway before distance learning — and interactive video in particular — was heralded. What *is* significant is that delivering training which is truly responsive to the student's learning needs and establishes an instant interactivity with him or her, can only serve to accelerate the trend towards learner centred training. Even more fundamental is the notion that the corporate culture is increasingly receptive to individualized learning, therefore training which uses interactive video and remote CBT is both in alignment with, and helping to promote, the prevailing philosophy and staff development. No matter how effectively designed and sensitively used, without this response of a supportive upper management, distance learning is unlikely to have anything other than superficial impact on the effectiveness of an organization.

Shaping the Future

Much of the emphasis in this review of strategy has been on the Training department responding to local training needs, stimulated in turn by customer demand. The second strand of distance learning strategy has an equally profound but more proactive edge. Profound because it relates to the very rationale of a training department being central to the success of a company. Proactive because the initiatives it launches seek to anticipate and even shape the future business environment. In many ways the pursuit of distance learning could appear very threatening to those involved in the design and delivery of conventional training courses. Inevitable questions loom in the minds of tutors and administrators: What will my role as a trainer be when a full range of distance learning packages is available?; If the responsibility for the training and development of staff is being taken up by local line managers, how will a central training function operate... indeed will it be necessary? It should be remembered that it is not an 'either or' situation. There will always be a place for conventionally run courses because — as we shall discuss below — some subject content is not appropriate for distance delivery. Nevertheless, such expressions of insecurity are not difficult to understand. Certainly a period of uncomfortable change will accompany the development and launch of distance learning programmes, but there are a number of good reasons why this tortuous transition may actually establish the Training department in a position of strength rather than undermine its influence as feared.

Enhancing Trainer Professionalism

For any training course to be effective it needs to be preceded by some form of training needs analysis. This is particularly the case where distance learning media are to be used, with the relative immutability of material once produced and the heavy investment costs at the outset in producing CBT and interactive video (in conventional programmes the major costs are incurred at the delivery stages). It is likely, for the same reasons, that fairly senior levels of management will be required to sanction budgets and release resources for the distance learning project in hand. The implication then is for the Training department to be involved as much in training consultancy as delivery. The determination of future business needs, the diagnosis of organizational problems, the discussion of appropriate strategies including training media, the cultivation of managerial commitment to embark on a plan of change to address the salient issues, will all be activities called for if the implementation of distance learning is to be effective. This close consultative process can only serve to heighten operational awareness of the Training department and the catalytic role it can play in organizational development.

Another way in which the profile of the Training department will be raised, is through the actual presence and accessibility of training courses locally. Whether the interactive video and/or computer based training work station be located in a dedicated learning centre or in a local BT business centre or even in an adjacent office, the opportunity to pursue a need-related development programme becomes that much more immediate both in terms of proximity and responsibility. There is always the tendency for the value of training programmes administered at a distant residential centre to be diminished by their inconvenience, mis-timing and, perhaps most significant of all, by the loss of autonomy the student experiences. There is an impressive body of research which correlates commitment to a course of action with the original freedom to choose that option (Kiesler 1971; Salancik 1971). If an appropriate range of training modules is available locally, the opportunity for self-determined development is enhanced, thus not only increasing the potential impact of the programme on the individual, but also involving his or her line manager more actively; and the sum total is to heighten local operational awareness of the central training function.

Building Trainer Skills

But what of the skills gained from this learner-oriented style of training? The most obvious are the job mastery skills addressed by the training programme itself. The provision of training or re-training opportunities in a local, self-paced, interactive learning environment increases both the breadth and accuracy of impact. More people can take advantage of the facility, and — in addition — key senior managers can be targeted in a way that the constraints of conventional delivery do not always allow. The potency for desired organizational change is therefore that much greater. Less obvious are the spin-off benefits for the Training department. Close involvement in the planning, design and production stages of a distance learning programme can help to refine and cultivate skills among existing tutors and training staff. Indeed it can be seen that disciplined and monitored work of this nature with carefully selected teams of trainers over a concentrated period of time is a very effective way for the department to carry out its own organization development. The kinds of skills developed would be: consultation abilities in the initial discernment of operational and training need; thoroughness and precision in the setting of module objectives; expertise in the selection of media appropriate for different types of programme content and desired outcomes; deeper understanding of educational design; negotiation skills in contracting with external producers and agencies; psychological awareness in the devising of validation tests and user response feedback, together with the analysis and use of this data. While these gains are not exclusive to distance learning development, the rigours of such a project, namely, the tight time and resource allocation, the versatility of learning media and the need for utmost clarity of instruction to script writers and visual designers, do intensify the appropriation of these and other skills.

These then, constitute the strategic objectives of a company committing itself with appreciable zeal to advanced technological media for the delivery of training. The picture of a piñata has been counterpoised with that of pandora's box to highlight the potential risks of such a venture. The strands of the training strategy can be summarized on three levels. On a *pragmatic* level, the Training department has a unique demand to respond to, in terms both of quality and of throughput of students, from a geographically dispersed hi-tech business. That demand has prompted the search for novel training solutions.

Computer based training, and especially interactive video, promise to assuage the demand without compromising on quality and, taken over the longer term, in a cost effective manner. On a *professional* level, the Training department provides a better quality and more efficient service to the business, and re-skills itself in the process, taking on more of a coaching and consultancy role to accompany the traditional tutor-based teaching. On a *philosophical* level, distance learning provides the vehicle for facilitating organization development: by putting quality programmes in the hands of local trainers it encourages line responsibility for field training; by ensuring that these programmes are accessible and interactive it reinforces student-centred learning; and by continuing its dialogue with and advice to local management it enhances its credibility and quality of service to the business. By doing these things the training function will move, imperceptibly but surely, from being perceived as a distant and peripheral activity to one which is at the hub of the organization.

Each of these potential gains from the piñata of distance learning is matched by at least one less pleasant outcome from Pandora's box, but these negative consequences derive less from the strategy itself than from the manner in which it is implemented, which is the subject of the next section.

Surfing Safari

Corporate strategic objectives may be entirely attuned to the external environment and responsive to internal pressures, but unless formulated into plans, they are futile. What follows is a review of some aspects of the plans for implementation of distance learning in BT. Specifically the need to manage expectations is touched on, then the decision to produce some interactive video programmes is described, followed by an explanation of why the particular topics were chosen. Finally some of the lessons learnt from the design and production phases are documented to illustrate the far from smooth working out of the new plans.

Managing Expectations

In many respects the plan BT adopted for introducing distance learning resembles, to coin the Beach Boys' golden song, a surfing safari. A safari because it was a pioneering venture and, as such, organizational precedents were scarce. Surfing because successful implementation was deemed to be dependent on managing to balance on a fast moving wave of opinion and rumour concerning CBT and interactive video. In other words a major element of the plan addressed the climate of opinion at different levels of the business. There was a need to create a sufficiently favourable general awareness of what distance learning could deliver, without raising expectations so high that the ultimate products were disappointingly few or inferior. The outcome would be disastrous either way. To spring distance learning programmes on the business before the appropriate infrastructure and all-important local commitment were established would have predictable results. On the other hand, to nurture local management so that they had high anticipation of what distance learning could offer them and their staff and then be unable to provide for their demand for training should also be avoided.

The Decision to Produce

It was decided that the best way to ride the cusp of this particular wave was to launch into the production of a number of existing management courses for delivery by interactive video. This plan avoided several of Pandora's pitfalls. It meant that BT as an organization could evaluate the virtues of the medium first-hand, without relying on the promotional accolades of producers. It also enabled BT to pursue instructional excellence and find the technology for authoring and delivery which least compromised these. The plan was also a way of silencing those critics who complained of training solutions being driven by high technology with more regard for sophisticated (and expensive) features than the integrity of the programme and the needs of the students. A further pitfall avoided was the passive one of simply spectating, and drawing conclusions based on the experience of other companies venturing into distance learning. To have taken such a cautious stance would have cost the Training department its proactive, consultative role, so central to its strategic objectives as discussed above, and would have cost BT its leading influence in the interactive video market place.

Rationale for Choice

Against that background, the six interactive video programmes described earlier were commissioned during 1985. Each one was chosen because in our view the subject matter lent itself to the virtues of interactive video treatment and the programme met a pressing need in the current management training profile. The Marketing and Network programmes, for instance, constitute modules in the week-long management induction course and had the added benefit of consistently exposing new managers to interactive video as a medium they might wish to harness in the future. Quite different was the Octara programme, which was aimed specifically at the BT Sales force, where interactive video was chosen because of the need simultaneously to appraise several hundred sales staff at locations throughout the UK on the facilities of a new key switching telephone system. As against the other programmes this one had a relatively short shelf-life, apart from refresher training (which indeed proved to be a distinct advantage because the launch date of the system was delayed) and induction training for new sales managers. A further interactive video was designed primarily for point of sale use within one of BT's telephone shops. By working on a number of programmes at a similar time the intention was to maximize our learning as a company about how to make good quality interactive video material. Apart from the project manager and subject expert, a training consultant with background in psychology was allocated to each project, his role being to facilitate the customer-client relationship, to advise on instructional strategy, to design and conduct evaluation, to document the learning process and so on. The decision was made to commission production companies for all the stages beyond preliminary design. Choosing four different producers for the six programmes enabled some useful comparative appraisal to take place. Each BT project team worked as closely as possible with the external producer through each stage up until disc pressing.

Lessons Learnt

As anticipated, the learning curve was steep, especially on the first few projects, and eight of the more important issues are enumerated here. First is the apparently elementary task of defining course objectives. This proved to be a time consuming phase of planning, partly because we were unclear of precisely what behavioural and skill outcomes we wanted to achieve or they evolved as time passed, partly because the production companies have different ways of soliciting and interpreting such objectives, and partly because of the media itself. While learning objectives should naturally be defined with precision at the outset, since validation will be related to these, the affective nature of interactive video does not actually encourage over-prescription at the outset (Lindsey 1984). Much of the value comes from idiosyncratic effects and linkages which individual students make, and it is not easy or even appropriate to anticipate these with strict programme objectives. This is particularly the case for attitude level material designed to increase students' motivation.

Second, when approaching external agencies for help it was found to be important to draw up a specification document at an early stage. This included statements about the design and integrity of course material, and the student support facilities required, a section on visual and audio technical standards, and licensing and marketing parameters. It is tempting to enter a contractual relationship with a supplier prematurely, before there is unanimity from the sponsors on course content and objectives, but if these are at all vague much costly time will be wasted.

Third, once the specification is agreed the contract can be put out to tender to a number of known suppliers and the competitive proposals assessed on the basis of content, approach, cost and time schedule. However, the resultant proposals are only likely to be substantial in design terms or precise in cost terms if the original specification from the company is comprehensive. Alternatively the customer could contract a few trusted suppliers for a research and development stage. These would cost around £5,000 each. Or the customer would contract one, two or possibly three suppliers for courseware design and video script. These would cost up to £10,000 each, but would yield a rich range of design possibilities and produce a very accurate second stage budget.

Fourth, the relationship with the contracted supplier could prove to be delicate, evolving and possibly long-term. For these reasons BT found it necessary to define clearly from the outset the roles and responsibilities of their participants, and to secure a corresponding commitment from the supplier.

Even though the point comes when the sponsoring organization 'hands over' the content and objectives to the design team of the production company to perform their creative wizardry, close monitoring is necessary to ensure the message is not being unwittingly distorted, the learning points are remaining intact, and the overall image and integrity is in accord with corporate philosophy. There are not many producers yet who have a detailed appreciation of the potential of interactive video media *as well as* its capabilities for effective instruction. The tendency therefore is to arrive at a basically linear, albeit entertaining, programme. Making the most of the media of interactive video calls for inventiveness at two levels: the overall approach to the material, including student choice of pathways, the varied and engaging use of case studies, simulations, games and so on; and secondly, the effective use of questioning techniques, with creative branching taking the student down new learning paths.

Fifth, a number of options are available for testing retention, learning and understanding *within* the programme. Once again, these need to be decided upon at an early stage since they can be integral to the flow of material. Measuring skills mastery 'back on the job' is more difficult but is possible given sensitively devised instruments.

Sixth is the crucial point of integrated design. Suppliers' conventions differ, but it should be insisted that some pictorial explanation be given of how *all* the different elements (visual images, voice-over, graphics, programmed text) interrelate with reference to the learning points. This will include a detailed flowchart showing all possible branching. Without a document of that nature it is difficult to assess the interactivity as against the linearity of the programme. Naturally, the project manager needs to be available throughout this stage for consultation. In particular he will be required to check what existing in-house material may be used and ensure smooth access to customer buildings, equipment and facilities.

Seventh, most programmes will require some form of support material, to reinforce and supplement the interactive video programme. Decisions need to be made concerning the depth, technical quality and desired connection with the main material. Once again it should be the project manager who regularly reviews progress, checking particularly for screen design conventions and degree of interactivity, as well as overall 'flavour'.

Finally, the stages of production are usually carried out under tight time constraints because the disc pressing facility has been booked months beforehand. Despite this urgency it is crucial for the customer to review the final version of the master tape prior to pressing and duplication, simply because it is an irrevocable and costly process. Special attention should be paid to the visual quality (checking for such things as dropout, and bleeding) and audio quality (checking for noise to signal radio, intermodulation and so on).

Those were some of the learning points which emerged as the design and production schedules materialized. Some were anticipated but many more were not, and for this very reason the basic plan to monitor and evaluate interactive video at first hand seems to have been well justified.

Enabling Structures

Organizational plans concerning the introduction of interactive video were discussed above with special reference to how the design and production schedules materialized. But plans need to be translated into structures, to enable the organization to progress forward a step at a time in alignment with the overall strategic objectives.   One of the   points of Child's   model is that the nature of these structures will be contingent upon a set of influential factors, like the history of the company, its diversity of operations, the prevailing technology and the characteristics of its staff (Child 1977). Although what is efficacious for one company may be quite unsuited to another, examples of four enabling structures which BT devised will be cited below.

Standards

The breadth and diversity of operational units within BT, many of them eager to explore and harness the benefits of interactive video for training and/or point of sale applications, called for early agreement on company standards: which hardware configuration to choose; what was the most effective and pertinent authoring and delivery software. Similarly, externally produced courseware was vetted for use within BT and intelligence gathered on the quality of video producers and external consultants. This coordinating and standard setting was felt by the Training department to be an important regulating function, ensuring technological compatibility within the company and excellence of service from the market place.

Criteria for Training Media

Managers and trainers in BT have often asked whether CBT and interactive video are appropriate media. The answer to this question depends on two others: What is the desired outcome of the training? and Who is the audience? If the educational intent of the programme is informational, in other words the simple exposition of a message, then interactive video could be employed, but visual images in the form of a linear video, or even straightforward text, would suffice. If the content concerns the awareness of procedures and accompanying mechanical skills, where it is important to check on job mastery, an interactive mode which challenges the student actively to demonstrate understanding is called for, especially if the next time that task is performed it is on an expensive piece of equipment, or in front of a key customer. What about the deeper level of training that tackles employee attitudes? Here the affective nature of interactive video is a powerful and persuasive tool, if designed well. However, it is probably not sufficient to achieve desired results on its own. The trainer would want to follow up the programme in a face to face situation, and possibly also involve the student's line manager to ensure that the ideas have taken root.

Another crucial consideration is who the target audience of the training is. Whilst it may be inappropriate, on grounds of cost if nothing else, to design an interactive video programme for one sub-audience alone, it may well be that the same core video material is relevant to many other people in the business, given a different pathway through the programme. This could be a prime case for using the versatility of interactive video. For instance, interactive video courseware specifying the features of a new product could provide excellent training for the sales force, maintenance engineers, customer liaison staff and even customer point-of-sale training, given some skilled instructional script-writing and programming by the design team.

Judgement Matrix

The above factors have been summarized on a judgement matrix, a form which enables a potential sponsor of a new training programme (or a manager wishing to convert an existing course) to assess speedily whether CBT or interactive video treatment would be effective for the kinds of student outcomes envisaged. The matrix, based on what little research has been so far conducted on training media comparison (Clark 1984) and on a range of key operational questions, like timescales, target audience(s), shelf-life and so on, is an example of another structure designed to facilitate the effective implementation of distance learning. Indeed, accompanied with such a matrix a training manager who had hitherto dismissed distance learning, may be stimulated to explore the use of CBT or interactive video for his or her courses.

Consultancy Papers

Following on from the matrix the Training department have put together a number of consultancy papers to assist and guide BT managers who are embarking on interactive video projects. The papers are a consolidation of the learning gained over a year's involvement with the medium, gleaned from the project logs and diaries of the project managers, subject experts and psychologists seconded to the respective interactive programmes. Assuming that a client BT manager has at least a preliminary understanding of the medium, gained from either the permanent distance learning display at the Training department headquarters or through one of a number of demonstrations and workshops held locally, an overview paper is provided which highlights some of the more significant implications of interactive video training. This would include a project overview of the different parties involved in the design and production of interactive video (see Figure 9.2). If the training needs diagnosis phase does indicate that interactive video would be an effective strategy the distance learning consultant will take the manager through a sequence of further papers which give more detailed guidance on the setting of technical specifications, on tendering and contracting, and on the resource allocation needed for design and production, as well as the licensing and marketing of the finished product. Once again, this is intended to be a structural mechanism for helping a speculative project move forward to fruition without relearning lessons from the past.

Conclusions

By reflecting on British Telecom's experience I have sought to address the question posed in the title. It was noted how the Training department's strategy was forged from a number of elements: the history of involvement with distance learning, influential events in the external environment and the internal dynamics of an organization in metamorphosis. Some aspects of the plan and structures for implementing locally delivered distance learning were traced. Those structures naturally translate into a number of activities which, though not discussed here, are in turn evaluated and fed back as internal performance information which closes the cycle by moulding future strategic objectives. Appraisal of performance, comprising careful evaluation of the interactive video programmes so far produced, is the stage now reached by BT.

Central to the cyclical model of organizational performance is the quality of management. Which returns us to the theme running throughout this discussion. Whether the use of distance learning media generally and interactive video in particular, shower benefits upon the organization in the way a piñata should, or whether, conversely, they serve only to open the lid of pandora's box, depends very much on the managerial skill with which the implementation is handled. If senior management are attuned to the internal and external pressures upon their business and if they are confident that the broader corporate culture supports the shift toward individualized instruction, then it is more likely to succeed. If the strategic plan effectively manages the expectations of the business by both building organizational momentum and meeting demand for local training when it comes, then the evils of training solutions imposed from above and unrelated to operational needs will be avoided. If mechanisms are constructed which are appropriate to the history, staff, technology and size of the corporation and enable managers to move painlessly into the field of distance learning, then not only will business performance be enhanced but the training function itself will have established its credibility for the future.

In the experience of BT so far the benefits of investing in distance learning far outweigh the potential problems.

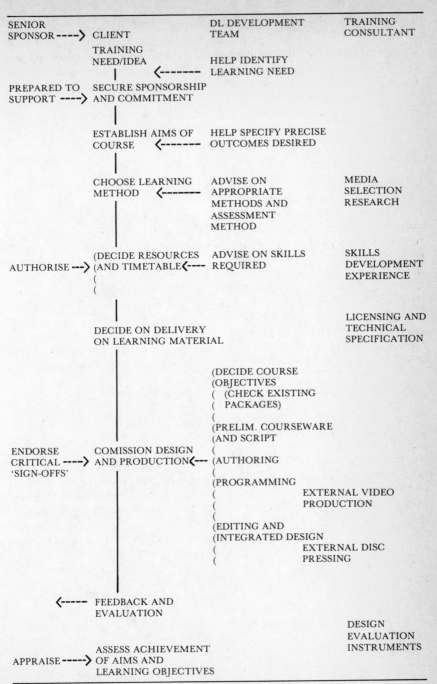

Figure 9.2
Project overview of interactive video production in BT.

Acknowledgements

This article is based on the hard won experience of many colleagues and my thanks go to them all, especially to Dr Scott Kerr for his critical reading of the first draft.

10

Community Education and the Limits of Openness

Angie Ballard

Whose needs are you meeting?
Are you talking about open access or open learning?
How far are you an agent for change and how much a palliative for the masses?
Why must you be self-financing?
Why are you part of the Open University and not an Open Tech project?
How can you deal with painful or emotional subjects in distance learning materials?

The six questions above are some of those put to me during a presentation of the Community Education Programme at the Open University and of the strategies that have been used both to extend access and increase the openness of the programme's material. Some of the questions reflect concerns we have ourselves and debate periodically or worry about incessantly, others brought a fresh perspective to our situation.

Philosophy and Purpose at the Open University

Community Education at the Open University offers flexible distance learning material at a non-degree level in a variety of subject areas intended to meet the functional needs of adults. Currently there are twelve courses and fifteen packs offered (Open University 1985) 'to help people with new stages in the life cycle – having and bringing up children, looking after elderly relatives, approaching retirement, or with changes in the environment or with roles in society' (Open University 1984). Provision ranges from *The First Years of Life* and *The Pre-School Child*, the first two courses to be presented in 1977, to *Racism in the Workplace*, a study pack first available in 1982, and the latest offerings in 1985 which are *Healthy Eating* and *In and Out of Unemployment*.
The Open University's charter states:

The objectives of the University shall be the advancement and dissemination of learning and knowledge by teaching and research, by a diversity of means such as broadcasting and technological devices appropriate to higher education, by correspondence tuition, residential courses and seminars and in other relevant ways and shall be to provide education of University and professional standards for its students, and to promote the educational well-being of the community generally. (Open University 1969)

Community Education was set up to meet the last requirement, following the Venables Committee recommendations in 1974. As that committee stated:

more of the same is not enough – to increase access we must have different forms of provision in wider areas. (Venables 1976)

Briefly, the overall goals of the Community Education Programme are:

1   To meet the learning needs of individuals at various stages in their lives: in their roles as parents, consumers, employees and citizens, in the context of their family, workplace and community.
2   To reach as wide a range of learners as possible regardless of prior educational achievements, through appropriate learning materials and support for their learning.
3   To collaborate with national and local organizations in defining needs, developing learning materials, sharing resources, publicising and promoting learning opportunities, organising support for learners and in evaluating the provision.
4   To finance this work, within the rules laid down by the University, from student fees, external grants and other sources of income. (Calder and Farnes 1981)

Lamentably, the present financial policy of the University is for Community Education to be self-financing. The programme has been partially funded by outside monies, and the ten years' support from the Health Education Council is particularly noteworthy, having shaped the direction and orientation of much of the work. (Calder and Ballard 1983; Farnes 1979, 1984; Farnes, Ballard, Jones and Baines 1986).

The Context

Community Education is one of six programmes making up the University's Continuing Education provision. The others are Health and Social Welfare, Personal and Cultural Education, Science and Technology Up-dating, Management Education and Professional Development in Education.

A wide variety of courses and resource materials are offered within the Continuing Education provision, ranging from a 50p poster to over £800 for a specialized scientific course and its home experiment facility. The 1985 Continuing Education Guide separates out three main strands of provision:

'courses to help further a career'

'courses to develop personal interests'
'family and community courses' (Open University 1984)

Courses offered within each of these six programmes, or sectors as they are called within the OU may be courses from the undergraduate programme or newly generated material. Such material may be offered in a formally structured way, with assessment, to make up a course, or as resource material, available with little contact with the university. In the case of Community Education, both sorts of provision are offered, as for example the Health Choices course, and the Look After Yourself discussion pack which was derived from it. Most of the Community Education material is in the Health and Parent Education area, but there is also material for personal and community workers.

Community Education is thus one part of Continuing Education which, together with the massive undergraduate programme, and the much smaller higher degrees programme, makes up the total provision of the university.

The Open University was created on the initiative of the Labour Government of the day with the aim of providing educational opportunities for adults who wished to study in their own homes and in their own time. The accepted view is that it was intended primarily for those who had missed out on educational opportunities in the past or did not possess the normal university entrance qualifications, and Woodley traces the development and history of this unwritten tenet (Woodley 1981).

There are no entry requirements and admission is on a 'first come first served' basis. The first 25,000 undergraduate students began their studies in January 1971. Since then a total of 180,000 have been admitted and 70,000 degrees awarded. Around 20,000 new undergraduate students are admitted each year, and there are nearly 70,000 currently studying at any one time. In addition, Continuing Education has some 30,000 'students', and since 1977 there have been over 250,000 users of Community Education material.

There are areas of commonality between the Continuing Education and undergraduate programmes as shown in Table 10.1. But, as Table 10.2 shows, there are some fundamental differences too.

	CE Programmes	UG Programmes
Access/ Constituency	Open to all adults (minimum age of entry varies)	Open to all adults (normally 21 years and over)
Locality	National	National
Major teaching mode	Distance teaching	Distance teaching
Medium of instruction	Multi-media	Multi-media

Table 10.1
(From Calder, O'Shea and Bailey 1985)

	CE Programmes	UG Programmes
What they're trying to do	Meet learning needs	Communicate knowledge[1]
Who they're trying to do it for	Anyone with the specified learning need	Anyone capable of coping with the intellectual demands
How they're trying to do it	'Long' and short courses, course packs and resource material packs for people with varying lengths of experience in a wide range of areas of need	Structured 'long' courses at different academic levels in wide range of subject areas
How success is judged	Normally by the application or implementation of skills or knowledge acquired	By mastery of course content as shown by the award of a credit

[1] Colleagues working in the undergraduate area have protested that this is too much of a simplification of the complex process of studying within the Open University, usually for a degree.

Table 10.2
(From Calder, O'Shea and Bailey 1985)

Criteria for Success

With the Open University's national delivery system, Community Education material has the potential to reach a mass audience, and we know from our evaluation studies that, with varying degrees of adaptation, it has successfully reached audiences ranging from the semi-literate to the postgraduate. But there are limitations — both with the format and the delivery system itself, and with the institutional context in which we operate. The University requirement to be self-financing and the tensions between on the one hand providing education as a subsidized service available to all and on the other a commodity competing in the market place impose limits on what is achieved.

The following reflect some of the working knowledge and shared philosophy found within Community Education:

— the learner is *aware* of the provision
— the material is *accessible* both in terms of price and format
— the material is *relevant* to the learners needs
— the learner receives *support* from the inherent structure in the material and from other people (Calder and Farnes 1981; Williams, Calder and Moore 1981)
— the *outcomes* from interacting with the material are perceived as valuable by the learner: people with negative experience of current educational provision should not have their self-image further damaged but should be given confidence to value their learning drawing on their life experiences.

But what happens in the real world? How many of our potential audience do we lose at each stage? The above five facets may be seen as a distillation process, and we know much more about the final stages than we do about the first. The following concentrates on what we know; making estimates of the loss of our potential audience at each stage is not an exercise we've undertaken yet — but hope to do so in the near future.

Awareness

Community Education, as we have said, is only a part of the Open University's provision. Not surprisingly, awareness of the Open University has increased since it was established: in 1971 a Gallup Study showed 31% of the population were aware of the University, rising to 83% in 1983. However, in 1983 only 36% were aware of the Community Education part of it (Swift 1981). The material provided by Community Education, with its optional assessment, runs counter to the image of the 'Open University producing graduates'.

The Community Education Catalogue and the Continuing Education Guide are two attempts to provide potential learners with a clearer picture of what Community Education courses are like and where they fit in the overall pattern of Open University provision (Open University 1984, 1985). But the potential learners are a heterogenous group, a spectrum with individual learners studying on their own at one end and institutional purchasers, buying material for their client group, for use in a training course, or to have for reference, at the other end (Williams, Calder and Moore 1981; Calder et al. 1979; Stainton-Rogers 1983; Hurley and Gearing 1983).

Where our prime target audience are and how we best make them aware of what is available is a continuing debate. In 1986 the Catalogue is being specifically targeted for institutional users or intermediaries. They may be buying the material to use directly themselves or to pass on to others in their organization. The individual learner, in contrast, will be informed via a Prospectus, which lays stress on course provision.

The objective set in the 1986 Plan for Community Education (Farnes 1985a) is 'the promotion of learning opportunities' which is interpreted in the broadest sense both of other agencies and learners in direct contact with the Open University using the material, either centrally or via regional offices. It is hoped the more clearly defined targeting of publicity and promotion of material will not only increase awareness, but uptake as well. Thus for 1986/1987 there will be a revised catalogue for intermediaries and professional users entitled *Learning Materials for Community, Adult and Health Education 1986/1987, Resources for Learning and Discussion Courses for Professional Development* and a prospectus for individual students provisionally entitled *Learning for Living*.

Accessibility

If the learner or user is aware of the material, is it accessible? Can they afford it and is the format such that they can easily use it?

In the nine years since the first material was available in Community Education, there have been over 120,000 participants in the programme, whilst 135,000 books from the courses, published by commercial publishers, have been purchased by the general public (Farnes et al. 1986). In addition, there has been extensive use by professionals and para-professionals such as health visitors, health education officers, midwives, social workers, pre-school playgroup association members and child minders.

The first two courses had some 12,000 registered students and although aimed at parents, 95% of these were women — a marked contrast to the undergraduate programme. However, their educational background was similar. For example, less than 10% had no educational qualifications compared to 8% of undergraduate students in 1977 and 6% in 1971. About 20% had left school at the earliest opportunity compared to 30% of the 1977 undergraduate students, and 23% in 1972. We knew for the first presentations that a minimum of 5% of Community Education 'students' were professionals wanting copies of the material to use in their work, but in 1977 the only way of obtaining material was to register as a student, so we were not reaching 'as wide a range of learners as possible regardless of prior educational achievements' (Ballard and Dale 1985a, 1985b; Lilley and Calder 1978).

Early evaluation work identified confidence and motivation as hurdles for the less educationally experienced, and price as a hurdle for many (the courses were £9 in 1977, and in 1986 will be £29.95, having been £30 in 1985) (Calder and Ballard 1981). Two specific attempts to improve accessibility have been:

1   The Sponsored Places Scheme
2   Varied presentation of the material and its format to widen the appeal.

To see if barriers of price, confidence and motivation could be overcome, the Health Education Council in 1978/1979 provided funding for a pilot scheme of sponsored places on The First Years of Life, aiming to reach disadvantaged learners. Material was distributed via sponsored place organisers, generally health visitors. The scheme successfully demonstrated that those with little experience of formal education could make full use of the material and, more importantly, that the majority of those participating felt they benefited from the material, particularly in terms of increased confidence (Calder and Ballard 1981).

The scheme was extended to include all HEC funded material and the Scottish Health Education Group have provided funds too, whilst the Strathclyde Open Learning Project and the Open University Foundation and Unemployment Scheme also provide direct sponsorship for learners.

In 1978 the proportion of students with no formal qualifications was between 17 and 21% for sponsored places, compared to 7% for fee paying students. By 1984 the proportion for sponsored place students was about half, and in 1983 nearly three-quarters had left school at the earliest opportunity (Ballard and Dale 1985b).

However, the HEC sponsored scheme in its present form will end in 1986 with the end of the five-year funding. It is hoped the university will provide for some limited continuation of the scheme (Farnes 1985b); a cynical view is that Community Education acts as the public social conscience, similar to Boot and Reynolds' 'Kept Radicals' (Boot and Reynolds 1984b).

One of the major changes in provision since the first two courses were presented in 1977 has been the move away from providing 'courses'. Early feedback revealed the constraints of specific study times, with potential students having to apply at fixed times to study over a fixed period.

Rolling mailings were introduced whereby in principle people received material within three weeks of ordering and could study when they liked. This was followed by rolling admissions, so that applications were accepted for most of the year, and the final phase has been rolling assignments — those people who opt for assessment are given a wide choice of dates by which to submit their material.

In 1977, to obtain material people registered for courses, which included optional assessment. Today people purchase study packs from the Learning Materials Sales Office and opt into assessment if they so wish by purchasing the assessment pack — and 'registering for assessment'. Those wanting the material for information only or as resource material thus gain access without 'becoming students' (Calder et al. 1979; Stainton-Rogers 1983; Hurley and Gearing 1983).

The course texts were originally designed as two- and four-page topic spreads so that they could be off-printed as 'leaflets'. In one early experiment in 1978/1979, 165 health professionals wrote in to request over 7500 sets of free leaflets over a period of only six months. No formal publicity had been given to the scheme (Calder, Shields and Lilley 1980). The success of the scheme encouraged other leaflet projects and led to the development of sets of discussion packs derived from course material (Ballard 1982; Ballard and Spratley 1983).

Other attempts to exploit the course material included special booklets based on course texts written to accompany a number of independent local radio projects. Listeners to the specially devised radio programmes wrote or telephoned in to their local station for the free booklets. To date, results are mixed. Over 1100 listeners to Pennine and Birmingham stations wrote in for The Pre-School Child (Lilley 1980). In contrast some 3000 wrote or telephoned for Pre-Retirement, which was offered by sixteen different radio stations.

However, other developments would seem to have made the material less available. Only one course is still broadcast; since 1984 all other past TV material has been available only on video. The impact of this has not been fully assessed, but it would seem to be a retrogressive step (Kirkup 1985), even if undertaken only for reasons of economy.

Relevance

Both the content of the material and the processes used in study need to be relevant to the learner. Each topic is designed to be a self-contained learning experience dealing with a particular set of issues. The material is interactive structured learning material, ie includes devices which get the learner to:

— examine their own experiences, values and resources
— organize these to make decisions, and
— take appropriate action.

The process the learner engages in transcends the direct content of the material.

Figure 10.1 is a page of text from Health Choices (Open University 1980) illustrating the 'key elements' found in Community Education text:

— An introduction presenting relevant facts, raising key questions, and outlining the way the topic will look at the issues.
— Questionnaires to help learners explore their own feelings and ideas, and reveal the way they normally approach issues.
— Activities to help learners to sort out what is important to them, weigh up different approaches and make decisions. Often activities are arranged in a sequence where learners' responses to one activity feed into the next.
— Feedback sections to provide comments on the learners' responses in the activities.
— Examples to show how a variety of other people have tackled the same questions.
— Case studies and quotes to show how the issues affect other people and how they tackled them.
— Information boxes to provide useful facts and information in a clear and concise form.
— 'What Next' boxes to give ideas and information to take learning further (Farnes et al. 1986)

Needless to say, not all pieces of text exhibit all the features that this selected sample does.

The content of the material has to be seen as relevant, either to life stage or to role in the community, and material is available on:

parenting
health
consumer choice
energy conservation
governing schools
unemployment
racism

But whose needs are we identifying and meeting? The collaborating agencies and funding bodies have their goals as well as the Open University. Final control over the academic content rests with the University, but the strength and mix of the collaborating agencies give us the pattern of courses and packs found today.

On a more general level, Community Education itself wishes to broaden the base and nature of collaboration. In a recent personal note appraising the development of Community Education, Calder made the following observations:

— The range of provision — at present, six out of the nine short courses and six out of the eight study packs are in the health/family education area. This is clearly too high a concentration in one area.
— At present only two courses, Racism and School Governors, are concerned with facilitating change and development within the community as opposed to the individual.
— Thus for the future: A wide range of collaborators should be sought, including unions, charities, pressure groups and established community groups. (Calder 1984)

Concern to produce material relevant to needs resulted in the Van Leer project, which worked with community based groups to generate material. The project resulted in a pack of materials, Women and Young Children, but along the way raised fundamental issues about Community Education and how our predominantly print-based *at a distance* format would compare with grass roots Community Development work (Lambers and Griffiths 1983). It was from this work, together with the Topic Leaflet Experiments, that the group discussion packs emerged — material provided as a resource for discussion groups and not individually focused.

Support

Support for the learner or other user is provided both by the inherent structure of the material, described above, and by personal support: the help, encouragement and often added enjoyment of sharing experiences with others. When the First Parent material was presented in 1977, a system of voluntary local co-ordinators was established to put students in touch with one another. On the first presentation of the courses, about half the students intended joining a self-help group and between a fifth and a third of those made it to a meeting: often there was no meeting as there were no other students nearby, although some students were very enthusiastic and one student in Scotland did a 100-mile round trip to attend (Calder and Lilley 1979).

As the number of courses increased, it became clear some rationalization of the centrally organized network was needed and in 1983 the management of the five hundred plus co-ordinators was decentralized to the Open University Regional Offices (Woodley, Ballard and Sayer 1984a). Further pruning of budgets has led to the present system where local contacts are operated by the Regional Offices together with focused collaborative project. There are local agencies, especially local authorities and community outreach projects.

INTRIGUER

WORKED EXAMPLE

You're more active than you think!

Some health campaigns imply 'If only you were more active

your problems would vanish.' But can exercise cure all your ills?

MOTIVATOR

How active are you?

You still have many opportunities to be active in your everyday life even though there are many labour-saving machines at work and in the home and most travelling is done by car, bus or train. By looking at how you spend your time you can find out just how active you really are.

Vigorous activity

Our everyday activities can be divided into four grades according to how vigorous they are.

Grade	Examples	Your activities
A No conscious activity	Sleeping, lying down	
B Minimal activity	Sitting down, motorway driving	
C Light activity	Standing while doing something, eg, shaving, washing-up. Moving around a bit, eg, sweeping the floor, washing the car	
D Vigorous activity	Brisk walking, gardening, scrubbing floors, polishing furniture, washing clothes by hand, light manual work, active love making, climbing stairs, running, cycling, most sports, heavy manual labouring	

WORKING KNOWLEDGE

Think through your day and grade your activities in this way, then fill in the boxes in the chart. You will need to have another look at your grade C activities later on in this topic.

But now you should concentrate on your grade D activities because if you do a total — not necessarily all at once — of 30 or more minutes each day of grade D activity then you probably have all the exercise you need to keep physically fit.

It's only grade D activities that count. Doing more of a less vigorous activity doesn't have the same effect on the body. Vigorous activity gets your heart pumping fast and hard which it needs to do each day.

Try to keep a diary for four days. Two week-days and a weekend will give you the most useful information. If you've got a good memory you can note down at the end of each day all the Grade D activities you did and how long you spent on them, or you may find it easier to keep an accurate record if you make a note each time you do a grade D activity. Here is Jane's diary:

ACTIVITY INSTRUCTIONS

Jane's Diary

Activity	How long
Date Fri 13th	
Walked — fairly fast — to the station to go to work	*20 mins*
Walked round shops at lunch time	*15 mins*
Walked home from the station — carrying the shopping	*25 mins*
Cleaned up the house like mad for the weekend	*25 mins*
Total	*1 hour 40 mins*
Date Sat 14th	
Gardening — did the lawn with a hand mower	*20 mins*
Emptied out the kitchen cupboards, scrubbed them out, put all the things back. A lot of bending and stretching!	*55 mins*
Total	*1 hour 15 mins*
Date Sun 15th	
Walked round the park after lunch. Just about brisk enough for Grade D	*40 mins*
Total	*40 mins*
Date Mon 16th	
Walked to the station. (Didn't walk home at night, got a lift home from the station — it was pouring with rain.) Didn't do any housework in evening, watched TV	*20 mins*
Total	*20 mins*

On most days Jane gets 30 or more minutes of vigorous activity. She is busy and active often just walking to and from work or doing the housework. However, getting a lift to and from the station each day would cut out most of her vigorous activity!

In your diary your days' scores will give you an idea of how your weekday activities compare with your weekends. You can also see, for instance, how much that game of football on Tuesday, or walking to work when the car was laid up, increased your score. Remember, to keep fit you should be doing 30 minutes (or more) of a grade D activity every day. About one hour on three or four days a week would probably be just as good.

Jane, for example, reckoned she could offset her Monday score against her against her vigorous Friday. You need to keep the score balanced within the week. One week's holiday — say, pony-trekking — won't offset three months of sitting down at a desk all day and in front of the television at night!

Do you need to do more?

Did you find that you don't usually do enough vigorous activity? To do enough isn't nearly as bad as it sounds. You don't have to take up a special exercise or sport. You can become more active through quite small changes in your life. The following list shows the energy saving way and the more active way of doing some common activities. Place a tick against the 'active ways' you already do and an asterisk (*) against those you *could* do.

PERSONALISED FEEDBACK LEADING TO DECISION MAKING

ANALYSIS WORKED EXAMPLE FEEDBACK

IMPLEMENTATION
OF CHANGE

MONITORING

You may have a good reason for not being able to do some of these activities in a more active way. Think of some of your other activities that you *could* put more energy into doing.

Easy way

Take the lift or escalator
Take the bus or train
Shopping trolley on wheels
Spray polish the furniture and floors
Wash clothes in washing machine
Tumble dry washing
Use an electric drill or saw
Buy and cook convenience foods
Amuse children by turning on TV
Ask your workmates/secretary/partner to fetch and carry for you
Power mow the lawn
Your examples
a
b
c

More active way

Use the stairs
Cycle or walk all or part of the way
Hand held shopping bags
Hand wax polish the furniture and floors
Wash clothes by hand
Hang washing on line and iron it
Use a hand drill or saw
Buy, prepare and cook fresh food
Amuse children by playing with them, taking them for walks
Get up and do it yourself!
Hand mow the lawn
a
b
c

You probably realise that most of the things we suggest mean going back to an old way of doing things. You may think this a waste of time and would rather have time free for more exciting things than chores. Fine. But if you do want to be more active then you will have to use some of your spare time on exercise or sport.

Being fit

A leading fitness expert has suggested that in addition to this vigorous activity the average person needs to:
● twist and turn the major joints through a full range of movement each day to keep the body supple. (Most grade D activities would do this.)

● stand for a total of two hours a day, not necessarily at one time, to help the circulation of the blood and put stress on the bones to maintain their structure.

To check if you are standing for a total of two hours a day you may need to go back to the chart of the four grades of activity. All grade C activities are done standing up. So are most of grade D activities (except vigorous activities like cycling and rowing).

It should be quite easy for you to do more grade C activities if you need to increase the time you spend on your feet.

● each day lift a heavy load for at least five seconds to maintain muscular strength. (Be sure to lift carefully and bend your knees rather than your back when you lift.) Just lift ordinary objects such as a full shopping bag, a typewriter, a basket load of wet washing, an average suitcase or a small child.

SUMMARY AND
'WHAT NEXT?'
INFORMATION

To sum up ...

It is not hard to get fit and stay fit. It really doesn't have to be a difficult and unpleasant process. This topic has shown you how doing enough of your everyday activities can keep you fit. But if you can't — or don't want to — make your working day more active you might like to do a simple, properly planned set of exercises (see the next two topics). Or you might like to increase your activity level by taking up a sport, in which case *In the swing* in this chapter will help you choose what to do. As long as you choose the right form of exercise, begin slowly and work up gradually day by day, week by week, you'll gain all the benefits without straining yourself.

Figure 10.1
Extract from *Health Choices* (Open University 1980).

Notable examples of such projects have been the Strathclyde Open Learning Experiment based in Glasgow and the Manpower Services Commission project in the South East, with 130 Community Development Officers providing learning opportunities for on average forty learners. The success of this has led to a national scheme to include 400 Community Development Officers (see Best 1984; Woodley et al. 1984a, 1984b; Dolley 1984; Burd and Barmeister 1985).

The change in emphasis from support for self-help groups to support for local groups came about partly because of the University's deteriorating financial circumstances but partly because of the obviously increased and enhanced effect of the Regional Offices' *local* contact with communities compared with the distanced, centralized and national system.

Outcomes

The 1986 Review summarizes the outcomes reported by recipients in a number of studies:

— Knowledge gain was cited as the main benefit by between 65—70% of fee paying and sponsored students. It is also claimed as the main long-term benefit by 49% of students.
— 90–94% of students felt that the recent courses had added to their understanding of children.
— Enhanced skills is the second most common type of long-term benefit for students.
— Between 63–70% of students on the early parenting courses reported some attitude changes in themselves.
— Increased self-confidence was reported as a major benefit by 20% of parents and other users of the parenting courses.
— Changes in practice: over 50% of parent course students reported changes in the things they do with their children and a similar proportion of pilot Healthy Eating students reported changing their eating habits to follow national guidelines.
— Professionals in health and other caring professions have evidenced considerable satisfaction with the flexibility and usefulness of course materials in their own work.
— Participating in local groups has provided an added direction for many learners, increasing enjoyment and boosting confidence and self-esteem.

More feedback on outcomes for the individual comes from the often lengthy comments included by students and material purchasers, and the following two quotations were both freely volunteered in the most recent pack purchases study:

I just thought it would be interesting because my child is about the right age for the course and I just thought I'd like to know more about what you could be doing and it's given me more confidence before she goes to playgroup for instance — what she could be doing in the meantime.

I have been working as a full-time Community Worker with the national organization for the past six years, and I start my Community Diploma course in September of this year. Ten years ago I was a bored housewife. I joined a YMCA playgroup, at which I was encouraged to take part in an OU course on Under 5s. This was a turning point for me, as I realized there was so much more I wanted to learn. Since then I have attended many courses and seminars on a wide range of topics, ranging from Drug Abuse to Counselling. Although I have not taken part in any other OU courses, I believe it is an excellent avenue to reintroduce people to education and learning. I have used the recent packs I purchased with a Womens Group, and although it is not used in a formal manner, I believe the women have learned and grown as individuals through the use of the OU materials. Maybe in the future they will decide to take advantage of the credits system, but in the meantime they are still gaining from the OU materials. (Ballard and Mason 1986)

As well as benefiting individually, users share their material and pass on copies. A longitudinal study of students on The Pre-School Child showed 31% shared material, whilst over half (54%) had passed the material on to others — the overwhelming number to friends (Ballard and Dale 1982).

Issues and Implications

Community Education material has the potential for reaching many, but what is realistic? We can reach the masses but can we reach them economically? What are to be our criteria for success? Too often success is viewed in terms of numbers, rather than in terms of the experience engendered for the users of our material. Commenting on an earlier version of this paper, the Director of Community Education agreed that the quality of experience is known from early evaluation studies and continued reports from organizations, students and users reinforce this belief, so that the issue becomes one of scale and mere numbers. Are the Community Education participants an addition to the estimated 5% engaged on 'educational courses of a substantial nature?' (Woodley et al. 1983).

We are in the anomalous position of knowing less and less about our users because of changes in administrative practices and access routes within the Open University. The flexibility of access and several pathways into studying Community Education are developments to be encouraged, but that very flexibility precludes some of our earlier 'knowns'. To take two examples: first, how many of our purchasers are also users of the material? In a recent study of institutional purchasers, a tenth were going to use the material themselves, but all reported that the main intended use was with others at work, either with one group or several groups, and nearly a fifth were using material as the basis of a training course. In contrast, of individual purchasers nearly half had sent for material for their personal use, a tenth intended using it themselves in their job, and a fifth wanted it for use with or by others.

Secondly, with regard to sponsorship — we know that the number of people directly sponsored through formal OU schemes was over 31,000 to the end of 1985. However, people are also sponsored by their employer or another agency — the 1985 study showed that between a quarter and a half of purchasers in one year were sponsored that way and not through formal OU schemes. What proportion of learners are wholly financing themselves, how has this changed since 1977, and what would be the impact of raised fees (Ballard and Mason 1986)?

Working with Community Education one becomes familiar with the unanswered, and in some areas unanswerable, questions of the sort set out at the beginning of this chapter. First, whose needs are we meeting? We attempt to meet individual's needs as well as the Open University and collaborating agencies' goals by producing material that is personally relevant to the learner and gets them to review and value their experience. Such material does not meet the needs of those looking for prescription or for advanced technical discussions of topics.

Second, are we talking about open access or open learning? We have undertaken a number of projects to increase access to the material, such as sponsored places, the encouragement of informal and alternative uses of material and other adaptation and dissemination projects. We have done less systematic work on open learning, which the material certainly does allow for by offering learners a choice of routes through it. But there is currently debate within Community Education about the pros and cons of this approach, and some argument in favour of more strongly linear material with little choice of routes.

Much of the evaluation of developments, based in an institutional research setting, has concentrated on open access. Should resources permit, both the evaluators in the Institute of Educational Technology and Community Education would welcome an opportunity to do the more detailed work on the quality of learning as exemplified by work done by the Study Methods Group on the Social Science Foundation course (Taylor et al. 1983; Gibbs et al. 1980).

The use and effect of the interactive materials in areas such as parenting, health and, most recently, changing eating patterns, is of particular concern, especially in view of the self-reported changes from developmental testers of the material (Bailey 1985a, 1985b).

Third, how far is the OU an agent for change and how much a palliative for the masses? The material encourages questioning and testing of ideas, but the impact of over a quarter of a million people using the material in some shape or form over a nine-year period is not known. To become more of an 'agent for change' we need more provision in the community area.

In addition, the loss of formal support of the self-help groups has weakened our links with what does happen in the community. Our SOLE project, with 1075 receiving joint Strathclyde-Open University Certificates, presented at a special ceremony by the Vice-Chancellor in June 1984, shows how, when used in conjunction with other agencies, Community Education provision can indeed have impact on the community (Woodley et al. 1984b).

Fourth, why must you be self-financing? The institutional and political climate in which we operate demands self-financing of Continuing Education:

it is additional to the undergraduate programme that is the raison d'être of the University. Welsh offered some trenchant criticisms of the 'self-financing' principle:

> If the Vice Chancellor is serious in his call for CE commercial viability then steps along the above lines must follow. Anything short of autonomous management by commercial professionals will leave CE in its present position of a subsidised, cosmetic gesture to concern with continuing education provision. Commercial viability demands commercial performance and this cannot be achieved in the present university context of CE and its relationship to the remainder of the Open University. (Welsh 1983) (see also 1981, 1982)

Continuing Education has been able to achieve self-financing status, but Community Education with its commitment to the educationally disadvantaged, in trying to hold fee levels to a minimum, and with its sponsorship schemes, has not.

As the Director of Community Education has stated:

> Recognition of the Open University Community Education programme has reached an all time high through the grants awarded in 1984, and 1985 will exceed this. The range of courses and packs is extensive and their use widespread. However, in nearly ten years of development it has not proved possible to achieve complete self-financing, even with cuts to the major activities. The future for Community Education, without a relaxation of the self-financing principle, looks grave. However, agreement on this (i.e. relaxation of self-financing principle) and the recognition and support of others will enable Community Education to continue to meet the functional learning needs of adults regardless of their educational qualifications and economic circumstances. (Farnes 1985a)

To date, Community Education have argued their special case and have received indirect support from the other areas of Continuing Education but this is a matter for debate and negotiation each year.

Fifth, why are you part of the Open University and not an Open Tech project? The Charter incorporated the objective of providing for the educational well-being of the community generally. Being part of the Open University is a strength of the programme in terms of expertise and reputation, but can be problematic, for example in engendering a recognized identity for Community Education in the field.

Sixth, how can you deal with painful or emotional subjects in distance learning materials? The structure of the material and the extensive developmental testing normally undertaken has shown that such issues can be dealt with successfully — an area covered in detail in Chapter 5 above.

Times are changing, both in the University, where increased emphasis is placed on management education and scientific and technological updating, and in the outside world. How open, flexible and accessible Community Education will be at the end of a second ten years, or indeed if it is then still intact in its present form, is an unknown.

11

European Experience

Tore Aksjøberg, Magdolna Csath, Heinz Schwalbe and Sarah J. Mann

A Norwegian Model
by Tore Aksjøberg

The NKS Management School in Norway organizes the provision of management education leading to a national qualification, by means of distance teaching supplemented by classroom tuition. Three main problems are noted here: to do with the quality of the classroom tuition, the integration of the units of study and the quantity of the assignments.

Norsk Korrespondanseskole (NKS) was founded in 1914, the first correspondence school to open in Norway and the second in Scandinavia. Since then, more than two million have studied at the School, which in 1976 became a self-owned foundation. Currently NKS has between 80,000 and 100,000 active students, making it the largest correspondence school in Scandinavia, and one of the largest in Western Europe. It caters for a sizeable proportion of the four million people in Norway.

Besides having approximately 140 full-time employees (ie administrative personnel), NKS employs more than 400 part-time correspondence-tutors on a freelance basis. Many of these work in industry, commerce or other educational institutions. Among them are a wide range of professionals including psychologists, lawyers, engineers and economists. Their outside, up-to-date experience is regarded as extremely valuable.

Although the majority of NKS students are on courses chosen in order to pursue their private needs and ambitions, others are on courses used in personnel training programmes in business and public administration.

In Norway, all correspondence courses must be approved by the Royal Ministry of Education. Once approved they are also entitled to financial support from the government. Approval depends on whether the materials are judged suitable for study without the physical presence of a teacher. All students receive government support automatically through their correspondence college, without having to apply for it individually.

NKS offers students three modes of study:

— Individual correspondence tuition, working at home and sending in individual assignments to be marked and returned.
— Study circle tuition, in a group of between five and twelve students, discussing and working on a chosen subject and sending in a joint assignment.
— Combined instruction, involving classroom attendance at least one evening per week in addition to correspondence tuition.

The NKS School of Management

The NKS School of Management was founded in 1968, in response to an initiative from the Royal Ministry of Education to establish programmes suitable for managers in small and medium sized enterprises and middle managers in larger companies, aimed at increasing their understanding of business, economics and management. NKS was granted the right to develop and offer such a programme, and with the co-operation of the National Institute of Technology to award a public certificate to its students.

Approximately 3000 students enrol for the management programme each year, making this the most popular programme run at NKS. Following a co-operation agreement between NKS and the Association of Norwegian Engineers (NITO) in 1979, more than 3000 engineers have enrolled as students.

Students are scattered all over Norway and are adults in full employment, mostly with family obligations. Approximately 30% are women. The average age is around thirty, and all are assumed to have had between five and ten years of employment experience following secondary school level education.

The Management Programme

The management programme is aimed at those occupying or wishing to attain a managerial position in a small firm or a departmental management position in a larger firm. The intention is to provide knowledge relevant to such work rather than preparation for an academic career. The emphasis is on providing a useful 'toolkit' of applicable factual subject knowledge in business, economics, marketing, management and business law. Less emphasis is placed on the education and development of the person, except in a component course entitled 'Leadership: a challenge'.

Since 1980, following heavy demand from students, the professional title Managerial Economist has been given to those who pass the examinations. In our belief that the curriculum is post secondary school level we feel that that status is fully merited.

Students are required to complete the programme in one and a half years, ie in three semesters. The majority choose to study by combined tuition, although about 200 study by correspondence alone.

The ten component courses are studied in a prescribed order, three in each of the first two semesters and four in the third. Existing subjects cover areas of accounting, marketing, leadership, strategic management, labour law, economics and finance. Although the curriculum has been constantly updated, there is no coverage as yet of electronic data processing, which many students believe to be an important omission. In 1986 it will be offered during a voluntary fourth semester.

Responsibility for the curriculum rests with NKS, where all the learning materials are designed. These contain many examples and exercises, and a suggested study plan. Each is divided into several units, which serve to break the study down into manageable steps, with targets which do not seem too distant from where the learner is. Each unit ends with an assignment to be sent to NKS for comment and grading.

The correspondence school teachers from NKS are expected to give encouragement, control and support to students, as well as evaluating, correcting and marking work, and providing explanatory comments.

Classroom instruction, attendance at which is recommended for all students, is intended to supplement the correspondence tuition. It is provided by local, part-time tutors. The People's University, who are represented in almost every Norwegian community, provide 80% of the classroom tuition, the remainder comes from a variety of voluntary study organizations. Classes are offered at approximately 130 locations across Norway. For most students the arrangement is that they attend on one evening a week during each semester of 16 or 17 weeks. Evening attendance involves four classes, each of 45 minutes.

Attending a fixed schedule of classes is thought to help people to maintain progress and avoid falling so far behind that they give up. There is an element of discipline, albeit voluntary. The classroom teacher is expected to act as a resource person, whose task is to add to the subject matter, answer questions, and give special attention to parts of the topic in question which students find difficult. Their task is not one of lecturing. They may initiate and arrange discussions between students, who often have valuable knowledge and viewpoints to share. Often classes are divided up for such group work.

Classroom tuition is intended to provide motivation and impetus to continue studying. Classroom tutors usually have had broad experience of business life, and have received higher education in economics or administration.

The local organizers who employ the classroom tutors also make arrangements concerning the examinations, which themselves are set by the National Institute of Technology.

Problems and Achievements

In March 1983 we carried out a postal survey among students who had passed the final examination during the previous year. Only 5% expressed dissatifaction with the overall mode of studying as established by NKS, 25% replied that it was satisfactory, 50% good, and 20% very good.

The local part-time tutors received less favourable ratings than the NKS correspondence teachers and the materials, the former being judged by 15% to have performed badly, whereas only 5% gave that rating to their NKS teacher. Only 5% rated the material to have been bad. This emphasized what we had been aware of for some time, that the quality of the local part-time tutors, of whom there are more than 250, was variable. When evidence of poor tuition is discovered by NKS, an attempt is made to persuade the collaborating organization to replace the tutor concerned.

It is desirable to avoid the need to replace tutors, for it does nothing to help any students who have dropped out or whose classes have been dissolved. We feel however, that extensive training for classroom tutors would be too expensive. Instead, NKS concentrates on providing them with supporting materials to guide their teaching, and invites them to attend week-end conferences which take place three or four times a year. At such conferences, both curricula and pedagogic questions are addressed. However, only some 20 teachers turn up, so we are reaching only a limited number of them.

Another problem is that we are not fully satisfied with the way in which the separate courses are integrated within the one management programme. Each of them is constructed as an independent correspondence course, and there are cases of duplication between them as well as instances of unsatisfactory interconnection.

A third problem is that the school requires too many assignments, each of the forty-one of them demanding a substantial amount of work. Some students are unable to complete them all, and we believe that those students are less well prepared for the examinations, and get lower examination marks. We also believe that the quantity of assignments is a significant reason for many people dropping out, and that has serious financial consequences for NKS.

Overall, however, we believe that our model of education works reasonably well. We recognize that improvements are necessary, but take pleasure from the fact that 94% of those surveyed answered 'Yes' to a question whether the time spent with the School of Management was time well spent or not.

Distance Teaching for Management Development in Hungary
by Magdolna Csath

It is the development of distance teaching methods for management education in Hungary that is addressed here, the focus being on the reasons why distance teaching is being adopted, what has been developed, and the benefits and possible limitations which have become apparent.

Rationale

The Political and Economic Context

Since 1968 there has been a shift in policy towards increasing the competitiveness of the Hungarian economy within home and overseas markets. Until 1984, however, because managers were still accountable to the ministries which employed them rather than to the enterprise in which they worked, there had been little change in the way enterprises were managed in order to deal with the changing economic environment. The most recent reforms have made the majority of managers more directly accountable to members of the enterprises in which they work, which should enable them to concentrate on the demands of the business environment.

The main objectives of the latest reform are:

— to enable active adaptation by enterprises to a changing environment
— to increase corporate competitiveness and to achieve economic and technological success, and
— to increase living standards at the same time as increasing efficiency.

The means for achieving these reforms are through:

— developing the independence of corporate decision-making
— decentralizing organizations
— increasing the importance of small businesses and of officially sanctioned private sector activity, and
— reforming management practices in business.

In this political and economic context of change, management education has become crucially important. The economy needs more managers who are entrepreneurial, risk-taking and independent. The education system has to meet the economy's demands as quickly as possible with high quality and efficient methods. Distance teaching is one way of doing so.

The Management Education Context

Currently the main providers of management education are:

— The Hungarian Management Development Centre
— The educational centres of branch ministries such as the Ministry for Industry
— The universities

There are also some private consulting firms and in-company training centres in large companies which offer specific courses for immediate needs. Nonetheless, the current provision of face-to-face management education is small and has been concentrated on top and middle-level managers in large and medium-sized companies. The major bottleneck for progress in management education, especially for those in small businesses and for less senior employees in medium and large companies, is a shortage of competent teachers and trainers, while the economy needs a huge educational intervention aimed at managers at all levels. Given this shortage of teachers, which inhibits the scale of traditional face-to-face teaching, distance teaching methods have become an important resource.

Management Needs

There is a huge volume of diverse needs for management education in Hungary, and immediate action is required if the 1968 and 1984 reforms are to be effective. The nature of individual managers' needs is influenced by their age, their professional background, their managerial level, the size of the enterprise they work in, and by the means through which they have been appointed as managers. The main needs are:

i   the development of creativity, entrepreneurship and flexibility in order to promote effectiveness in dealing with a competitive market;

ii   attitude change, particularly among senior managers, aged between 50 and 60, who were originally appointed during the period of central planning before 1968;

iii   specialist subject areas, in particular economics, marketing and finance, for the large number of managers who do not have that professional background;

iv   job specific knowledge and skills at all levels in an enterprise;

v   managers working in state controlled industries enabled to cope with the now more competitive external environment; and

vi   strategic management skills to help managers deal with a rapidly changing environment in which they must anticipate future problems and opportunities and provide a clear picture of the goals of a company then convey these goals to all employees.

This classification reveals a spectrum of needs for management education in Hungary. The range of needs is not only broad but also requires immediate action if the 1968 and 1984 reforms are to be effective. Needs must therefore be met in both quantitative and qualitative terms: that is, as many needs as possible must be met in the most effective way. Distance teaching appears to be one of the means available to meet such pressing demands.

Distance Teaching for Management Education

Distance teaching has recently been used to support nation-wide objectives related to language teaching, computer programming and applications, and updating in biology, biotechnology and micro-electronics. All those programmes have been delivered via the national television network and, in the case of computing, have been supported by video-tapes, texts and access to local computer centres. There has also been a joint university and company initiative supported by the Ministry of Industry, to develop programmes for training in new machinery and new technology.

Recent developments have thus provided management education with a background of experience and expertise in distance teaching on which to draw. The following distance teaching programmes have been produced for management education by the Hungarian Management Development Centre:

— A package designed to inform managers of the new economic reforms being undertaken. This specifically addresses the new price system, new economic regulations, the taxation system, changes in corporate law, etc. The package includes a collection of cases and a series of video tapes, along with a concise guide book.
— A package on strategic management, which includes coursebooks, video-tapes showing cases from Hungarian industry, and audio and video tapes of presentations by Hungarian and foreign lecturers. A short course and opportunities for discussion are also offered as supplement to the package.
— Mini packages focusing on specific management methods and styles and on particular management problems, such as stress and ill health.
— The latest and most sophisticated development is a course for young managers-to-be, includes workbooks, guides, tapes and computer programmes for the students to work on when and where they wish.

There are also lectures at the Centre, visits to companies, and opportunities to work with a successful manager. Each student is allocated a tutor. The course lasts for ten months and is assessed by thesis and examination.

Three areas are currently thought to need a distance teaching intervention in the future:

i   Marketing and finance: It is assumed that only distance teaching can meet the huge demand for these subjects.
ii   The management of small businesses: In the last four years, 28,000 small businesses have sprung up creating a considerable demand for training.
iii   The training of non-managerial members of corporate councils in strategic decision-making.

Benefits and Limitations

We have not had enough experience with distance teaching methods to claim expert authority, but on the basis of recent activities we are able to summarize some benefits and some possible limitations in their scope.

The Benefits

Distance teaching makes a substantial contribution to the solution of educational problems. The following constitute the reasons why:

1   *Effectiveness*   Distance teaching can enable a relatively large number of

managers to be reached with urgency in order to introduce large-scale reforms, for example the Hungarian economic reforms.

2 *Flexibility*   Distance teaching can be easily adapted to individual needs; it is easy to combine distance teaching with other methods; and it is easy to meet new demands through distance teaching.

3 *Time and cost saving*   Only if done on a large scale will distance teaching programmes be cost effective. Time saving, on the other hand, is one of the most important benefits of distance teaching, especially for managers who cannot spare the time to join traditional courses.

4 *Focusing*   With distance teaching, it is possible to focus on topics which are the most important for achieving urgent policy goals within a short period of time.

5 *Convenience in building an educational system*   Educators are able to know the extent of the knowledge to be included in particular distance teaching programmes. This makes it easier to develop a system of programmes to meet continuing needs in an incremental fashion.

The Limitations

The potential limitations of distance teaching are:

1 Interaction, communication and delegation are all crucial management activities, and yet how can this human side of management be learnt at a distance by a solo learner?

2 One of the more useful elements of traditional management education is that of people learning from each other's experience. How can this be achieved at a distance?

3 Learning in traditional classroom environments takes place within a competitive atmosphere where there is never enough time for careful decision-making, evaluating potential projects, etc. This recreates a situation which is similar to that of real life. How can one re-create such an environment through distance teaching?

4 The real success of a distance teaching programme depends upon it concentrating sufficiently closely on the problems of the users. However, the more one attempts to meet the specific needs of small groups of users, the more expensive it is to develop a suitable programme.

5 Distance teaching — as it is currently provided — demands a special infrastructure, for example, the development of video tapes and computer programmes. This is expensive to build up.

Conclusion

As far as management education in Hungary is concerned, we have to go ahead with distance teaching methods since they seem to be the only way we shall be able to meet the demands of the economy. We may be able to tackle some of the needs which have arisen out of the recent reforms. However, we still need to consider ways in which we can meet the demand for training in the day-to-day, interpersonal aspects of management. Can distance teaching be used here, or do we need to find another way?

Distance Education for Staff Training in Germany
by Heinz Schwalbe

A model is described here for the design and development of distance education courses which my company in Zurich has developed from the experience of designing and implementing such courses for staff training and development.

Simply stated, what you have to do in developing a distance education course is:

First: analyse the job;
Second: define the objectives;
Third: develop material;
Fourth: implement instructions;
Fifth: evaluate.

I shall discuss what we believe are the important aspects of each of these stages and the ways in which we approach each stage.

Analyse the Job

In analysing the job we have first to ask the very important question: Is there any need for the course we are trying to produce? We have then to check existing training facilities against real needs and try and find out what distance education could do to improve the situation.

It is important to ask another question: Can we produce the course? Do we have both the ability and the money? Automatic success does not come to a project because it is supported by a lot of money. Much more important is how the money is spent. What really counts is careful planning and preparation with respect to practical needs, and concern to ensure that our plans are economically feasible.

Included in this phase is defining the target groups for the proposed course. In general almost everybody can make use of distance education at some time, but it makes more sense to decide which are the most likely groups.

Define the Objectives

It is important in designing a distance education course to be able to describe what students should be able to know or do after each lesson and at the end of the whole course. You have to define the objectives both clearly and adequately, and only then should you think about what kind of methods and media you should use.

Develop Materials

Before developing the materials we have to select methods and media. When we speak of methods we mean teaching functions used in a specific teaching situation. Teaching functions can be: differentiation and grouping; steering and managing; transmission and stimulation; feedback guidance; elaboration and evaluation. Each function can potentially be fulfilled either by the teacher in person or with the help of different media. In order to find an adequate method for a certain distance education course we are forced to select which function will have priority, as we cannot use all functions equally. However, we need to recognize all the functions, because finding the right method for a special teaching situation or a special course is less a selection process than a process of setting priorities in accordance with the objectives, the target group, and the kind of media used. In practice, conflict occurs between choosing the best method and the best medium, which often has to be resolved by compromise.

The medium can be defined in simple words as: 'the way in which information is transmitted', ie as the channel of communication. Written and printed material still remain the two most popular media in distance education. But tapes, records, slides and films are also acknowledged media, as are TV and radio systems. Other media such as computers are also becoming available for distance education in many countries.

The effectiveness of distance education, however, does not depend on using a large variety of media. Whilst other media may enrich the learning process they do not eliminate the basic need for systematic reading and writing in the development of the liberally educated person. Education should involve meaningful activity and the methods used should not be a one-way flow of information and ideas, with media that only give a small chance of feedback. The use of expensive media can only be justified if there is a positive effect on student learning.

What is actually required is to find an effective mix of methods and media which are both available and take account of the following: the objectives and the characteristics of the target groups; the social environment; economic, political and organizational factors; the subject matter and the coding of information; and lastly the budget.

After the selection of methods and media there is the actual course design and, in particular, course-writing. Nix (1985) suggests some techniques that can be used for preparing course material which is student-centred. These are:

— include essential information only;
— help students by using words and structures they understand;
— relate the content to the student's job;
— use meaningful graphics;

— go from the simple to the difficult;
— use analogies;
— go from the known to the unknown;
— emphasise key information;
— use short, clear titles;
— use reasonable text length;
— create an interesting first assignment;
— write for both men and women;
— observe copyright laws;
— manage text reliability. (p.15)

In addition, good illustrations will make difficult concepts easier, and can also make the text more interesting. It is also important to remove any detail that is not essential.

Test design is also a part of course design. Course or chapter review exercises and assignments are all used to reinforce course objectives.

Two-Way Communication

Any form of two-way communication has to be seen as having an additional function to that of the course materials, and not as a substitute for them.

Tutors are an important part of any two-way communication system and they must be both trained for the job and aware of what else happens on the course.

Tutors need to provide study guidance, support to their utmost the will, ambition and interest of the distance student, and help strengthen their decision to study. Every contact with a student, be it face to face, by telephone or by correspondence, is an opportunity to provide support. However, if tutors don't handle the tests that students send in with care, such support will be rendered less than useless. A true/false method of marking will not work; tutors must give feedback to students and encourage them and strengthen their belief in their own abilities.

Cost-Effectiveness

It can be seen that there are a lot of steps involved in building up a distance education course, and each step needs to be cost-effective.

However, cost-effective courses are not only courses which do not cost a lot of money to produce, operate and administer. Cost-effectiveness is often found — or not — in the course itself. It is possible for a course produced for low expenditure of time and money to be not at all cost-effective because its teaching is poor!

Implementation and Evaluation

This last part will briefly describe how we implemented and evaluated the distance education courses that we designed and developed for the Reemtsma

Group according to the approach just described. The Reemtsma Group is a German organization comprising several cigarette factories and breweries as well as some other businesses. In all, the group has nearly 12,000 employees. In the courses that we developed for them the intention was not just to transmit knowledge, but to try to strengthen the human position of the individual worker.

Each of the three courses was divided into units and each unit was in turn divided into lessons. A lesson is generally meant to be the learning material for one day. Each lesson starts with a short description of the intended learning targets and finishes with a short test. At the end of each unit is another test which the student submits for marking.

The initial evaluation of the courses was done by giving a sample of students a course pre-test and by obtaining feedback on the lessons and the course as a whole from them. On the basis of this evaluation corrections were made to the course.

As the courses developed they were made more widely available to other companies in Germany. Naturally we wanted to know how well they were received and how the students were getting on. Therefore, for two of the courses we sent out questionnaires to graduates. For the third course, however, we developed a new system of combining a short questionnaire with the test forms that students send in as they complete each unit. As a result we now get immediate feedback.

We feel that the fact that 380 companies other than Reemtsma have shown real interest and have put participants on our course proves there is a very good future for distance education in industry and business, and that there is a lot of scope for its use in staff development and training.

Note

In addition to the works cited in the text, I recommend the following: Berdichevsky (1975); Eurich (1985); Holmberg (1985); Lampikowski et al. (1975); Schwalbe (1972, 1973, 1977a and b); and Zander (1984).

Issues and Implications
by Sarah J. Mann

Issues

The three cases from mainland Europe presented above each illustrate a different social purpose for which distance teaching may be used. The Hungarian case shows it as a means of implementing economic, political and social reform, the Norwegian case as a means of professionalization for the management cadre, and the West German case refers to a distance teaching programme whose aims are claimed to go beyond the transmission of knowledge and include the strengthening of the human position of the individual worker.

Besides raising issues of social purpose within distance education, the cases also cover specific roles and functions and the relationship of these with more traditional means of education. Thus, the role of the teacher, the role of the classroom group, the role of materials and the design of distance teaching programmes are also considered here.

Social Purposes of Distance Teaching

The Hungarian case illustrates the role of distance teaching in government sponsored economic, social and political reforms that are geared to satisfying the current perceived needs of the country through a shift in management practice and to some extent in ideology. Distance teaching has been chosen as a means of implementing the necessary educational changes at management level because it is seen as being both efficient and effective for rapid change where the needs to be met are many and varied, and where the current number and level of appropriate teaching staff is limited. Furthermore, the presentation and content of the educational intervention can in this way be standardized to meet the perceived learning demands of the intended reforms.

The Hungarian case also refers to distance teaching as a means of disseminating information — via television — about new laws and regulations. In this role it is providing a public information service which is opening up access to usually complex and hidden information.

The Norwegian case, on the other hand, shows distance teaching being used to provide access to management education and opportunities to acquire professional status for a geographically dispersed and sparse population. Thus the programme discussed is opening up access to educational provision and at the same time establishing a profession, of 'managerial economists'.

The West German case adds a further dimension to the purpose of distance teaching in the work context: the intention behind the programme is claimed to be not solely the dissemination of job-related knowledge, but also, and especially, the development of the individual worker.

The three cases reflect a dual function for distance teaching: to *open up access* for the individual to knowledge, information, educational opportunities (and possibly their own development) in order to satisfy personal needs and interests; and *to reach* large numbers of 'key' people and ensure that they have the training and development which will meet the requirements of government policy or of a certifying body. Thus, distance teaching can be seen to have potential both for widening educational opportunity and public access to information and for bringing together educational provision and central government policy.

The Teacher's Role

The Hungarian case illustrates how distance teaching methods can be used to offset a lack of appropriately qualified teaching staff. Thus, a small number of suitably experienced people can be involved in the development of the necessary programmes but there is no need for large numbers of teachers to front the provision.

However, both the Norwegian and West German cases show clearly that materials are not enough. The support of the educational institution is needed for study guidance and to help motivate the students and support them in any problems experienced either in the content of the course of study or in the process of undertaking it. Tutors are needed also to mark assignments, and in a way which provides the students with ongoing feedback. There seems to be a strong argument for tutorial support in distance teaching provision.

If this is so, then the role of the distance teaching tutor and the training of such tutors are matters which need to be carefully considered. The Norwegian case shows how limitations in the resources available for training of part-time tutors can lead to dissatisfaction on the part of the students. If distance teaching is to become any large part of the national provision of education, then it is important to consider how the training of distance teaching personnel should differ from or relate to the training of traditional classroom teachers. One could argue that both types of instruction should be part of the professional training of any one teacher; in this way the trainee may be able to explore more fully their role by examining it both in the traditional classroom and as it relates to distance teaching. Expertise in both kinds of teaching role would in that way also be developed.

The Role of the Classroom Group

In the Hungarian case, the lack of any kind of peer group in which the individual distance learner can participate is noted as a problem. Without a classroom group the interaction, communication and delegation which are identified as important aspects of a manager's job are missing in the learning context. The opportunity to learn from other people's experience is lost and the competitive classroom environment which can mirror the real business world outside is missing. It is interesting to look at these gaps in the light of the Norwegian case which, through its provision of different modes of study, enables the learner to have access to just this kind of learning. Besides the option of straightforward solo correspondence tuition, two modes of studying at a distance are offered which involve a peer group of learners. The first is a study circle, in which students work together on a chosen topic and jointly send in the relevant assignment. The second involves combined instruction, where the student attends a class once a week but also follows correspondence tuition. Working together in groups in either of these different modes of provision does bring the individual students into contact with others in similar situations and enables them to share and learn from each others' knowledge and experience. It does, however, depend to some extent on the skills of the classroom tutor or group facilitator.

Thus, it need not be the case that distance teaching is only offered in one mode. But where combined instruction, study circles or any other mode of face-to-face contact is provided, both the tutoring function and the enabling structures necessary for the establishment of groups need to be carefully thought through and prepared for, along with any necessary staff training.

The Role of Materials

Two issues arise out of the cases as these relate to the materials developed for distance teaching purposes. The first concerns the limits of standardization and the likelihood of there being multiple interpretations of the same 'content'. Educational provision via distance teaching programmes does ensure that each student 'receives' the same content and the same presentation of the said content. Whereas in a traditional classroom situation the content to be taught (as pre-specified in a syllabus) will be mediated by different individual teachers with different styles and different interpretations of the syllabus. The attraction of distance teaching materials for the implementation of central policy is that control can to a large extent be maintained over the shape and content of the syllabus.

Despite this, individual students will themselves also interpret the materials they study, according to their own individual needs, purposes, background knowledge, attitude, etc., whether the content to be taught is presented directly through materials or is mediated via a teacher. Standardization can only be achieved for the materials, not for the student's interpretations of them. A mode of distance study which includes group work will further encourage the exploration of the content of the materials used.

A second issue concerns the extent to which distance teaching is only effective for the dissemination of factual, conceptual and abstract knowledge, and not for the development of experiential, interpersonal and attitudinal knowledge. It is an assumption and not a proven reality that when particular students are engaged in learning through one-to-one interaction with a text they will work only at a conceptual level, and will not examine it in the light of their personal experience and attitudes. Three points can be made here. One is that it is unlikely that students will not, at some level at least, bring to bear their own experience, values and attitudes when studying. Secondly, there is no reason why distance teaching materials should not focus on examining experience, values and attitudes through the educational design of the materials. Thirdly, as we have seen, it is possible to develop a mode of study which allows individual students to form study groups in which such knowledge can be developed — facilitated either by a tutor or by process focused materials, and by the students themselves.

The Design of Distance Teaching Programmes

Both the Hungarian and the Norwegian experiences point to a pertinent issue facing designers of programmes. Do design teams determine in advance the scope of a 'whole' programme and then break it down into interconnecting modules, all to be produced before 'release' of the programme; or do they identify discrete areas of need and develop coherent but separate modules, ready for use as they are produced, but running the danger of overlap when students opt to build up a programme for themselves by putting together a range of such modules. Given the first option it is likely to take time for the development of a particular programme, but it will be well planned and coherent. However, it may then be less easy to change in response to feedback from evaluation or to adapt to an individual's particular needs. The second option, on the other hand, is more likely to be responsive to comments and to special needs which arise from feedback, but may run the danger of repetition and overlap.

A second point (which relates to the issue of standardization) concerns the provision of advice to writers and designers of distance teaching materials. Advice which suggests that writers 'go from the simple to the difficult' or 'go from the known to the unknown' potentially misses a crucial point. Simplicity, complexity, the known, the unknown, etc. are all relative values. They are not absolute. The writer's sense of simplicity will not coincide with that of all users of the particular programme being written. Whatever the design of the programme, each individual will bring to it a range of different attitudes, assumptions, values, needs, purposes and background knowledge which will influence their interpretation both of the content and of the values and assumptions implicit in the programme.

This multiplicity of interpretations poses a challenge to distance education and to traditional education in two ways. The first questions the assumption that the transmission of knowledge and the testing of its learning is a relatively straightforward matter of clear dissemination and subsequent measurement of understanding. The second is a challenge to distance education designers and providers to capitalize on differences in interpretation and experience among students, and not to ignore or deny those differences. Differences of interpretation among students and between students and the tutor can be seen as sources of learning rather than as stumbling blocks to the student's grasp of what particular materials 'really say' (ie the message).

Implications

It is interesting to find that the issues just discussed all apply in some measure also to traditional classroom teaching. By distancing the teacher from the learner and by placing greater emphasis on the material produced and on the infrastructure in which to present these, distance teaching methods provide an opportunity for reassessment of current approaches to teaching and learning and of the educational theories and philosophies underlying these. Focusing on the development of distance teaching provides an opportunity not only to re-examine existing pedagogical approaches but also to question the scope and nature of the subject matter to be 'covered' and its relationship to the means of instruction.

Sponsors of distance teaching modes of study which do not involve tutoring and/or study groups may make the dubious assumption that a standardized message will be interpreted the same way by all students. This may well be a workable assumption in the dissemination of factual knowledge, where this is done with care and attention, but not in the teaching and learning of any other kind of knowledge.

The study group mode may be better suited to the sharing and discussion of different ways of making sense of subject matter, and in this way may to some extent contribute to the development of the individual and be suited to vocational applications. That is to say it may contribute to developmental dissemination (Boot and Hodgson 1985, Chapter 1). However, it is not clear what the limits are, if any, to the fullness of personal development by such means.

Distance teaching is potentially a very powerful medium, enabling access for a large number of students, and radically widening educational opportunities for large groups of people who would not normally be reached. It also has the power to influence the current level of skills and expertise of any one group of people in a fairly immediate and responsive way in order, for example, to meet government policy or current nationwide needs. Such potency makes the need to re-examine current approaches to education — including distance education — all the more urgent, in view of the right to education and personal development of every individual.

IV
BEYOND
DISTANCE TEACHING
TOWARDS
OPEN LEARNING

12

Beyond Distance Teaching Towards Open Learning

Robin S. Snell, Vivien E. Hodgson and Sarah J. Mann

Our intention here is to clarify current meanings attached to distance teaching and open learning both in theory and in practice, in order to show what we understand by going 'beyond distance teaching, towards open learning'.

We begin by examining distance teaching as it is most commonly conceived of and practised, and discuss the conception in terms of its potential for the equalization of educational opportunity and for the raising of critical awareness.

We then describe and discuss different examples of open learning. And we show how the traditional way of distance teaching is an example of one particular type of open learning, that associated with open access education.

We then show that a move can be made beyond distance teaching towards a type of open learning associated with the empowerment of the individual as a learner by abandoning the form of education founded on transmission and instruction and embracing that which is founded on each individual's right of access to the creating and questioning of their own and others' meanings. We assess the way in which the various ideas put forward in this book might move us towards that kind of open learning.

Distance Teaching

Distance teaching is commonly defined as teaching that takes place at a distance from the learner. Some of the constraints of traditional teaching, such as having to attend a class at a particular time and place, are thus removed. The various ways in which non-contiguous teaching is achieved characterize the differences among the providers of distance teaching.

Distance teaching is generally managed by an educational institution, which may take on one or more of four main roles: instruction, tutoring, assessment and counselling. It is taken for granted that the instructional role in particular will be materials dependent.

Thus in distance teaching, instruction usually involves the design, development and production of self-instructional materials, ie taking the decisions about what content is to be included in what order and through what media (eg print, audio, video, etc.), and about what activities are to be carried out by the learner.

Responsibility is taken by the institutional providers for the relevance to the learner of the knowledge to be learnt and for devising the method of learning. Part of the providers' role may be to design assessable assignments.

The tutoring role in distance teaching involves working with learners on their progress and on any problems they may have with the subject matter itself. Learners will be provided with feedback on assignments and on any queries brought to the tutor. The means for providing tutoring and the scope of the tutor role will be defined by the institution. For example, decisions will be made as to whether tutoring should be carried out face-to-face or via correspondence, how far tutorial contact can be learner-initiated or is bounded by the particular structures of the educational institution. Responsibility is thus taken by the institution for helping the students with their learning and for providing students with feedback on how appropriate their learning is.

The assessment role in distance teaching involves judging the relevance and adequacy of an individual's learning and giving it a value according to a set of criteria for which the educational institution takes responsibility. In many cases, the assessment of assignments will lead to some kind of certification which learners can use publically to represent their achievements on the programme.

The counselling role in distance teaching offers learners help with any problems not specifically related to their understanding of what is to be learnt. The style of counselling may range from prescriptive advice on study methods through to listening in a non-directive way as learners articulate their difficulties. As with all the other roles in distance teaching, counselling will be defined and structured by the educational institution. Counselling is seen as particularly important since learning at a distance poses particular problems for most learners at the outset, accustomed as they are to studying in a classroom environment.

In distance teaching the learning materials developed by the educational institution take over the responsibility for instruction from the individual teacher, and the means of instruction become centralized and depersonalized. The constraints of traditional teaching which are thus removed include the need to attend a class at a particular time and place and to follow what is being taught at the pace chosen by teachers according to their judgement of the class as a whole. Furthermore, the dependence of the learner on an individual whom they may not like or who may not like them, and other such personality and social factors are also avoided.

While the primary function of the materials is that of instruction, the roles of tutoring, assessment and counselling may be incorporated in them to some extent — introductory sections on study guidance may be included, for example, or self-assessment questions with specimen answers. However, the burden of the non-instructional work in distance teaching is still taken by tutor-counsellors and tutoring and counselling, while they may still be conducted at a distance, for example by telephone, do maintain direct personal contact with the learner. Assessment may or may not be personalized and is used to support instruction and validate learning.

Thus in distance teaching the teacher is separated from the learner and instruction is transferred from the individual teacher to the educational institution and to the materials, with tutoring, counselling and assessment in support, ensuring effectiveness. The main function of distance teaching is to disseminate knowledge through self-instructional materials. Although provider institutions may vary according to the emphasis afforded to tutoring, counselling and assessment and according to how they and instruction are delivered, dissemination remains primary. One could say that distance teaching is an example of a dissemination orientation to open learning (see Chapter 1).

Peters' (1981) definition of distance teaching as a form of mass education takes an understanding of the dissemination orientation further by likening the means of dissemination in distance teaching to an industrial production process. Through distance teaching, the individual teacher's craft — which is available to a few at a particular time and place and which is supported by limited resources — can be standardized and made available to a large number of people by means of rationalization, the division of labour and mass production. Thus Peters defines distance teaching in the following way:

> Distance study is a rationalised method — involving the definition of labour — of providing knowledge which, as a result of applying the principles of industrial organisation as well as the extensive use of technology thus facilitating the reproduction of objective teaching activity in any numbers, allows a large number of students to participate in university study simultaneously, regardless of their place of residence and occupation. (p. 111)

Although Peters focuses particularly on the means of producing distance teaching, he also highlights its 'mass education' purpose. The translation of existing classroom-based educational provision into distance teaching programmes can provide educational opportunities for a greater number of people. In particular, distance teaching may enable people to have access for education who would not normally have done so. The Open University (UK) has amongst its goals to reach those who through lack of opportunity have been deprived of higher education, those who could not gain a place in conventional universities, and those large numbers of women who have not traditionally had either further or higher educational opportunities (Rumble 1982, p. 10). Perraton (1981) argues that distance teaching should be adopted as a means to expand education for egalitarian reasons. Young et al. (1980) state:

> In other words, education is to do with power. People without education are at the mercy of those with it, who can use what they know to their advantage

and to the disadvantage of the ignorant around them. Education is a means of gaining power, and not simply the right of the better-educated minority. On this showing the case for expanding education is a simple egalitarian one.

The innovation brought about by distance teaching has been the increase in access to traditional dissemination-oriented education through the removal of the need for learners to be in the presence of individual teachers. The traditional teacher role has been re-examined and new means developed of conveying knowledge to the learner. What distance teaching has not done is to re-examine the *dissemination* orientation to education.

Freire (1972) argues that education is not neutral. Its purpose can be either to 'domesticate' or to 'liberate'. Education domesticates where knowledge is given to or deposited into learners, where the relationship between educator and learner is that of subject to object. Education liberates where knowledge is 'born of the creative efforts of learners' (p. 24), those who are engaged in dialogue and critique with each other and an educator in subject to subject relationships.

Centralization in the educational institutions of the control of knowledge and depersonalization of the teaching role make it potentially harder in distance teaching for individual learners to question the value given to knowledge and gain power over it. It is a paradox that an increase in access to educational opportunity may result in a reduction of dialogue and questioning. That is, opening up access to educational opportunity through distance teaching may well not liberate as Perraton would wish, but instead increase the domesticating role of education. Does mass consumption increase our opportunity to be active and responsible subjects in the world or does it further alienate us by dulling our appetites?

Open Learning

On closer examination there are a number of different examples of educational provision and experience which can be thought of as open learning. We classify and describe each of these below and show how they differ.

Open Learning as Dissemination

Many existing definitions of open learning encapsulate the features of distance teaching which have been described above, ie as mass education through the widespread availability of self-instructional materials supported where necessary by tutoring, assessment and counselling. The emphasis is usually on the process of creating *open access* to education. The justification for open access is often given as the need to ensure that an adequately prepared and updated workforce exists for manufacturing and service industries. These commentators are adopting a *dissemination orientation* to open learning and see it as a matter of inculcating particular skills and items of knowledge in those who would otherwise not receive such education.

Stand Alone Dissemination

Stand alone dissemination is an attempt to build the four main roles of distance teaching into materials which will act as surrogate sources of tutoring, assessment and counselling besides instruction. Much of what is reported by Csath in Chapter 11 appears to exemplify this conception of open learning, as does Mabey's account in Chapter 9 of the interactive video programmes at British Telecom. Once the material is in the hands of the learner, the expectation is that no further contact with an education or training institution will be required.

Institution – Monitored Dissemination

Institution-monitored dissemination relies on an ongoing contact between tutors associated with an educational institution and learners. This arrangement is evident in the second case cited by Boot and Hodgson in Chapter 1, and in the case reported by Aksjøberg in Chapter 11. The teaching role is performed by the materials, with tutoring and counselling remaining a matter of personal contact with tutors, and assessment done other than through the materials.

In the case of community education programmes, reported by Ballard in Chapter 10, the provision of open learning can be either by stand alone dissemination or by institution-monitored dissemination. It is the latter if the learner chooses to register as a student, thus joining a programme involving ongoing correspondence for assessment purposes. Otherwise the materials can still be used as a self-contained programme. Perhaps this kind of flexibility of choice reflects a further erosion of administrative constraints on access to knowledge and is thus a sign of progress in open learning as viewed from a dissemination perspective.

Whatever the form of dissemination, emphasis is on the process of instructing the learner in a particular body of expertise. Open learning as dissemination is very much a matter of distance teaching. And it can again be asked whether or not such dissemination liberates the learners or domesticates them. The use of the term 'open learning' in the context of dissemination is suggestive of liberation. The learners' experience may, on the contrary, be of domestication.

Open Learning as Expert Networking

Self, in Chapter 6, and Rhodes, in Chapter 7, both imply that new technology provides further opportunities for advances in expert networking. This is a rather different conception of open learning from that of dissemination. The use of new technology as a vehicle for the sharing of discoveries, developments and reference materials among an expert network of peer specialists is similarly a matter of removing administrative constraints on access to information. The difference is that in expert networking open learning means sharing information among the members of an institution (which can be a profession), rather than handing down of information from the institution to the laiety, or turning laiety into able professionals. Materials associated with the expert network are regarded as reference sources rather than teaching materials. Thus expert networking (Rhodes suggests the term 'transactive system') is a move beyond distance teaching but is by no means a replacement for it.

Open Learning as Development

A radically different conception of open learning from that of dissemination or expert networking is one which emphasizes the development of the whole person and their ability to construct meaning in and through their lives. Boot and Hodgson in Chapter 1 term this a development orientation to open learning and give an example of it in the first of their cases. When conceived of as development, open learning is a matter of removing the constraints on a learner of being directed to learn about particular subject matter and to study in a particular way. Instead, the curriculum is open, individuals are encouraged to take on the responsibility for the direction and content of their own learning and for the processes of learning. The individual will have to learn how to learn (see Cunningham, Chapter 4) and to work with and through emotional pain and discomfort (see Snell, Chapter 5).

Institution-accredited Development

The particular case of open learning as development cited by Boot and Hodgson in Chapter 1 may be termed an example of *institution-accredited development*. Staff from the educational institution are involved not only as facilitators but also as the institution's representatives in the collaborative assessment process leading to the award of a recognized academic qualification.

Two schemes of independent study offered by the School of Independent Study at North East London Polytechnic (a Diploma in Higher Education and a Degree by Independent Study) also appear to be examples of institution-accredited development (Bradbury et al. 1982). Assessment procedures involve staff as unilateral judges of merit but the mode of assessment is open to co-determination by students. As part of their assessment some students have written novels, mounted exhibitions or constructed their own mechanical inventions. The exploration of theoretical ideas and knowledge is an integral part of the schemes, with the proviso that the student concentrates on how theoretical knowledge relates to cases which they encounter in practice. Another account of independent study schemes at undergraduate level which have a strong academic flavour is given by Percy and Ramsden (1980).

Students doing a higher degree by research, such as a PhD may also conceive of their studies as institution-accredited development. Rudd (1975) found that nearly half the PhD students he surveyed had entered graduate study predominantly because of an interest in a specialized field of study, an enjoyment of the process of doing research, or a desire to get a job as an academic. Development in this context appears to be a matter of developing a mature, lively and independent mind capable of conducting large scale, independent, original inquiry. Whether the development actually takes place seems to hinge on the student and on the quality of support given the student by supervisors, other staff members and fellow students.

Bennett and Knibbs (1986) suggest a number of ways in which the research supervisor can give the student support: by sharing expert knowledge of the field, for example, or mentoring on aspects of organizing and documenting the work done, by suggesting new ideas, providing friendly help and motivation or stern criticism, and by evaluation and judgement. If a balance of these is struck, then open learning in the sense of development will be engendered, with the student remaining free to determine the direction and content of their own learning in the course of doing original work.

Institution-supported Development

Other variants of a development orientation to open learning may place less emphasis than the foregoing examples on the evaluative role of educators. For example, Pedler (1986) discusses the role of management self-development groups. These may require a training specialist or educator to set them up and the support of the employer of the managers who are the learners in the group. Once commenced, Pedler suggests that the facilitator should seek early opportunity to withdraw, allowing the managers to continue unaided. Although the ideal of facilitator-less groups is seldom achieved in practice, there is no question of the sponsors or educators being involved in any certification process. Perhaps this could be termed *institution-supported development.*

Institution-supported activities are not always intended primarily to promote personal development but may nonetheless be a major source for it. Archaeological excavation work is one such example. Kenyon (1964) claims that although some of the work done by a volunteer on a dig can be somewhat dull or repetitive, with increasing responsibility the volunteer will develop the ability to take charge of more and more aspects of the work, culminating, if all goes well, in the opportunity to take charge. Wheeler (1956) and Woolley (1937) give accounts of what is involved in the management of an excavation. The image they convey is one of challenge, demanding the possession of or development of a wide range of qualities including scientific imagination, and the ability to manage all the different people on the excavation and their wide range of motivations. Whether initiated for the purpose or not, such expeditions are a rich source of institution-supported development.

Community Development

Fordham et al. (1979) describe how another variant of open learning as development evolved. Their brief as educators had been to increase the penetration of institutional adult education services in an inner-city area where formal educational attainment was low, as was participation in adult education. They recognized an alienation among members of that community from anything labelled 'education'. Although the educators retained some of their brief, and publicized traditional classes for adults, most of their energies appeared to go into promoting learning through action projects, and involving the members of the community in the production and distribution of a community magazine, in putting on their own social events, or organizing their own public meetings to identify and pursue better facilities for people in the community. The educators attribute much of their progress to their own willingness to work through existing 'gate-keeping' and political networks within the community and to work in the 'grey area' between adult education and community work. Perhaps this variant of open learning as development is best termed simply *community development*.

Deinstitutionalized Development

Other variants of open learning as development which are not associated with formal educational institutions may evolve through existing voluntary societies, social movements or simply through networks of friends. Examples would be groups of bereaved parents learning to experience and work through grief, women's groups engaged in consciousness raising or focusing on specific issues of health, safety or injustice, and writers' groups offering criticism, support and mutual advice on their writing. Without familiarity with the activities of any one particular group it would not be prudent to say whether their prime purpose was the development of their members, or was more to do with recreation and socialization, or was indeed the dissemination of information to members. Nonetheless, many of these relatively informal events are examples of open learning as development totally divorced from formal educational institutions, and may be termed *de-institutionalized development*.

It is a kind of open learning that has a long history. Illustrative is the tradition of 'mutual study, disputation and improvement' noted by Thompson (1965, p.743) as a strand of artisan culture in England during the early nineteenth century, which 'nurtured the values of intellectual enquiry and of mutuality'. He gives as an example of the activities associated with this the meetings of the London Corresponding Society, at which extracts from radical publications demanding social change were read aloud for the benefit of the illiterate, followed by ad hoc group discussion.

Development in a De-schooled Society

An ultimate vision of open learning as development is given by Illich (1973). He would disestablish all existing educational institutions. In their stead, would evolve new networks or learning webs, accessible to anyone motivated to seek the resources for education. One network would link industrial locations and neighbourhoods as living museums with reference centres and be a network of 'learning' objects. Others would be based on skills exchanges for mutual instruction, or peer-matching for joint inquiry and critique, and one would be a directory of independent educators and those who have used their services. Illich claims that the evolution of such networks would inevitably be accompanied by a profound change in society. One might therefore label his vision of open learning *development in a de-schooled society*. It presumes and encourages the mission of encouraging every citizen to take responsibility for the direction, content and process of their own learning. The erosion of formal educational institutions themselves (but not of educators) would mean that there would be open access to learning without the need for dissemination.

The above are some of the many possible variants of open learning as a process of development. None precludes the option of choosing distance teaching or even face to face teaching should the learner have need of it to meet a particular educational purpose. All of them go beyond distance teaching in that the mode of learning can extend beyond the reception of instruction or the discovery of predetermined findings towards genuine quest and discovery. Tutoring and counselling may go beyond encounter between expert and novice towards co-inquiry, comradeship and mutuality. Approaches to open learning as development vary according to the weight placed on the role of specialist educators, the extent to which access is readily available to people who wish to take part, and the extent to which people are themselves ready to take part in them.

Beyond Distance Teaching Towards Open Learning

The foregoing analysis demonstrates that in moving beyond distance teaching towards open learning we are moving beyond an educational approach with roots in the transmission and regularization of knowledge towards one with roots in the individual's creation of his or her own meaning and understanding.

The former approach tends to reflect a hierarchical image of society in which authority and power reside with those who are the holders and regulators of expert knowledge. The latter approach reflects a more open image in which everybody has both the ability and the right to create meaning and hold knowledge. It is all too easy for the proponents of the latter view to make the mistake of turning the right to create one's own meaning into an anti-intellectual endeavour that actively ignores the collected wisdom and thinking of others. Equally it is all to easy for the proponents of the former view to believe that their holding of knowledge gives them the right of power and authority over others.

The vision of people such as Illich, however, does not disabuse us of the importance and significance of the collected wisdom and thinking of others but advocates the greater sharing of this and the wider access to each others' knowledge and thinking. Such a vision is one of educational empowerment. Perhaps Illich's ideas are too visionary for them to be perceived by most as realistic. We do not have to be idealist visionaries, however, to see how some of the ideas arising out of the foregoing chapters could help to create a form of open learning which genuinely gives individuals the opportunity to develop in all senses and in what ever sense has most meaning to them. As Cunningham points out in Chapter 4 trainers and/or teachers cannot *not* influence. The issue is how we use our influence.

Cunningham himself believes that it is important to help learners to become aware both of how they learn and of the alternatives they have to their current patterns to learning. He sees learning 'problems' as resulting from the adoption of dysfunctional patterns to learning and suggests that there is no reason why a dysfunctional pattern cannot be changed to a functional one. He explains that learners often fail to adopt functional patterns to learning either because they do not even associate a given pattern with 'learning' or because they are unable to see how they can change one pattern for another.

Another potentially counter-productive experience to the process of learning is discussed by Snell in Chapter 5, who points out to what extent painful emotions can either prevent further learning or contribute to it. He concludes that painful emotions are frequently part and parcel of personal development. Consequently he suggests a number of strategies to help people deal with painful emotions in an open learning situation, his argument being that it is better to offer some strategies for dealing with such emotions than to let them prevent learning happening.

Strang in Chapter 3 similarly explains the significance of learners' own orientations to a course and points out the importance of helping learners to see what intrinsic interest a course may hold for them and why (if at all) it is important to them.

In Chapter 1 Boot and Hodgson label those approaches to open learning which have their roots in the individual's creation of his or her own meaning and understanding 'development oriented'. But a difficulty to be overcome in our attempts to move towards 'development oriented' open learning is that of the generally high cost of staff and resource intensive development programmes. New technology has been heralded by some as one answer, and the chapters by Self and Rhodes help us to consider what, realistically, it can potentially contribute to an educational provision which is more open. They both make it plain, however, that the technology is designed to make its biggest contribution in the storing and manipulation of large amounts of information. The implication is that the greatest potential educational function of at least some computers is that of the establishment and elaboration of accessible networks of knowledge rather than that of instruction.

We cannot say whether true *developmental dissemination* (Boota Hudgson) is in fact achievable or possible. But we believe that some of the ideas in this book can help us to move towards it. By conceiving of open learning in terms of developmental dissemination we may in fact achieve an educational provision that not only has its roots in the individual's creation of his or her own meaning and understanding but is also widely accessible and available.

REFERENCES

Anderson, J.R., Boyle, C.F. and Reiser, B.J. (1985) Intelligent tutoring systems *Science* 228, 456–462

Argyris, C. (1977) Double loop learning in organizations *Harvard Business Review* Sept–Oct 1977

Bailey, L. (1985a) *Choosing a Healthier Diet — Choices and Constraints* Paper presented at the 12th World Conference on Health Education, Dublin, September 1985

Bailey, L. (1985b) *Choosing to Change* Paper presented at the British Psychological Society Conference, December 1985

Ballard, A. and Dale, J. (1982) *The First Years of Life and the Pre-School Child — sharing the material — a preliminary note* CEEG Project Memo 41, The Open University

Ballard, A. (1982) *The PPA Leaflet Project* CEREG Paper No. 7, The Open University

Ballard, A. and Spratley, J. (1983) *Health Education Council and the Open University Look After Yourself and 'Health Topics' Project* CEREG Paper No. 15, The Open University

Ballard, A. and Dale, J. (1985a) *Community Education Digest of Statistics 1977–1983* IET, The Open University

Ballard, A. and Dale, J. (1985b) *Sponsored Places Student Demographics 1981–1983* IET, The Open University

Ballard, A. and Mason, R. (1986) *Community Education Packs Study. Preliminary Report* IET, The Open University (in preparation)

Bandler, R. and Grinder, J. (1979) *Frogs into Princes* Moab, Utah: Real People Press

Bandler, R. (1984) *Using your Brain for a Change* Moab, Utah: Real People Press

Bateson, G. (1972) *Steps to an Ecology of Mind* London: Paladin

Bennett, S.N. (1978) Recent research on teaching: a dream, a belief, and a model *British Journal of Educational Psychology* 48, 127–147

Bennett, R. and Knibbs, J. (1986) Researching for a higher degree: the role(s) of the supervisor *Management Education and Development* 17 (2), 137–145

Berdichevsky, R.V. (1975) Distance education — guided self-teaching *Epistolodidaktika* London

Berne, E. (1975) *What Do You Say After You Say "Hello"? — The Psychology of Human Destiny* London: Corgi Books

Best, J. (1984) *Evaluation of Support Materials for Community Education Collaborative Projects: a study of Strathclyde Open Learning Experiment* IET, The Open University

Biggs, J.B. (1978) Individual and group differences in study processes *British Journal of Educational Psychology* 48, 266–279

Biggs, J.B. (1985) The role of metalearning in study processes *British Journal of Educational Psychology* 55, 185–212

Binsted, D. and Hodgson, V.E. (1984) *Open and Distance Learning in Management Education and Training: A Positional Paper* University of Lancaster, January 1984

Blauner, R. (1964) *Alienation and Freedom* Chicago: University of Chicago

Boot, R. and Hodgson, V. (1985) *Open Learning: Meaning and Experience* Paper presented at Open and Distance Learning in Education and Development Conference, University of Lancaster, 1985

Boot, R. and Reynolds, M. (Eds) (1983) *Learning and Experience in Formal Education* Manchester University, Manchester Monographs

Boot, R.L. and Reynolds, P.M. (1984a) Rethinking experience-based events, In Cox, C. and Beck, J. (Eds) *Management Development: Advances in Theory and Practice* Wiley

Boot, R. and Reynolds, M. (1984b) Ideology in development *Management Education and Development* 15 (62) 183–187

Botkin, J.W., Elmandjara, M., and Malitza, M. (1979) *No Limits to Learning* Oxford: Pergamon Press

Brown, A.L., Campione, J.C., Day, J.D. (1981) Learning to learn. On training students to learn from texts *Educational Researcher* 10(2) 14–21

Boydell, T.H. and Pedler, M.J. (1979) Educational technology and significant learning? In Page, G.T., and Whitlock, Q.A. (Eds) *Aspects of Educational Technology, Vol. XIII: Educational Technology Twenty Years On* London: Kogan Page (pp. 349–354)

Bradbury, P., Hinds, E., Humm, M., and Robbins, D. (1982) Innovations in independent study at North East London Polytechnic. In Teather, D.C.B. (Ed.) *Towards the Community University: Case Studies of Innovation and Community Service.* London: Kogan Page

Bunderson, C. Victor, Olsen, Tames B. and Brillio, Bruce (1981) *Proof of Concept Demonstrations and Comparative Evaluation of a Prototype Intelligent Videodisc System* Learning Design Laboratories, WICAT Inc., Utah

Bundy, A. (1986) An expert system for medical diagnosis. In O'Shea T., Self, J., Thomas, G. (Eds) *Intelligent Knowledge Based Systems: an Introduction* London: Harper & Row

Burd, J. and Barmeister, C. (1985) *Evaluation of East Sussex Project 1984–1985* Community Education, The Open University

Burgoyne, J.G. and Cunningham, I. (1980) Facilitating behaviour in work centred management development In Beck, J. and Cox, C (Eds) *Advances in Management Education* Chichester, Sussex: J. Wiley

Burgoyne, J.G. and Hodgson, V.E. (1983) *Natural Learning and Managerial Action: A Phenomenlogical Study in the Field Setting: Journal of Management Studies* 20(3) 387–399

Burkhardt, H., Fraser, R., and Wells, C. (1982) Teaching style and program design. In Smith, P.R. (Ed.) *Computer Assisted Learning: Selected Proceedings From the CAL '81 Symposium* Oxford: Pergamon Press (pp. 77–84)

Burton, R.R. and Brown, J.S. (1979) An investigation of computer coaching for informal learning activities *Int. J. Man-Machine Studies* 11, 5–24

Calder, J., Lilley, A., Williams, W. and Baines, S. (1979) *Informal and Alternative Uses of 'The First Years of Life' and 'The Pre-School Child' Course Materials* CEEG Paper No. 7, The Open University

Calder, J. and Lilley, A. (1979) *Questionnaire Results for First Student Surveys* CEEG Questionnaire Results, IET, The Open University

Calder, J., Shields, J. and Lilley, A. (1980) *Topic Leaflets* CEEG Paper No.10, The Open University

Calder, J. and Ballard, A. (1981) *The Sponsored Places Pilot Scheme: an evaluation of the 1978/1979 HEC funded pilot scheme for sponsored places on 'The First Years of Life' (P911); a Community Education short course for parents* CEEG Paper No.13, The Open University

Calder, J. and Farnes, N. (1981) A distance learning contribution to community education. In Kaye, A.R. and Harry, K. (Eds) *Using the Media for Adult Basic Education* Croom Helm

Calder, J. and Ballard, A. (1983) *Health Education Council/The Open University Five Year Programme: A Review* The Open University

Calder, J. (1984) *An Appraisal of the Appropriate Development of the Community Education Programme at the Open University* IET Paper, The Open University

Calder, J., O'Shea, T. and Bailey, L. (1985) *IET Long-term Review Working Group, Continuing Education* Internal IET Paper, IET/EG/87/1A, The Open University

Capra, F. (1976) *The Tao of Physics* London: Fontana

Carroll, J.B. (1963) A model of school learning *Teachers College Record* 64, 723–733

Casey, D. (1985) The awful nature of change: motivation in hostile conditions *Management Education and Development* 16 (1) 14–16

Charniak, E. and McDermott, D. (1985) *Introduction to Artificial Intelligence* Reading, Mass.: Addison-Wesley

Child, J. (1977) *Organisation. A guide to problem and practice* London: Harper & Row

Clancey, W.J. (1983) Guidon, J. *Computer-Based Instruction* 10, 8–15

Clancey, W.J. (1984) Methodology for building an intelligent tutoring system In W. Kintsch et al (Eds.) *Methods and Tactics in Cognitive Science* Hillsdale, NJ: Lawrence Erlbaum

Clark, D.J. (1984) How do interactive videodiscs rate against other media? *Instructional Monitor*

Coffey, J. (1977) Open learning opportunities for mature students. In Davies, T.C. *Open Learning Systems for Mature Students* CET Working Paper 14

Colaizzi, P.F. (1978a) Learning and existence. Chapter 6 in Valle, R.S., and King, M. (Eds) *Existential and Phenomenological Alternatives for Psychology* New York: Oxford University Press

Colaizzi, P.F. (1978b) Psychological research as the phenomenologist views it. Chapter 3 in Valle, R.S. and King, M. (Eds) *Existential and Phenomenological Alternatives in Psychology* New York: Oxford University Press

Collins, A. and Stevens, A.L. (1982) Goals and strategies of inquiry teachers. In R. Glaser (Ed.) *Advances in Instructional Psychology Vol. 2* Hillsdale, N J: Lawrence Erlbaum

Cunningham, I. (1981) Self managed learning and independent study. In Boydell, T. and Pedler, M. *Managment Self Development* Aldershot, Hants: Gower

Cunningham, I. (1984) *Teaching Styles in Learner Centred Management Development Programmes* PhD Thesis, University of Lancaster

Cunningham, I. (1986) *Self Managed Learning in Organisations* London: Metacommunications

Cunningham, I. (in press) Self managed learning in action in Mumford, A. (Ed.) *Handbook of Management Development* Aldershot: Gower

Dansereau, D.F., Collins, K.W., McDonald, B.A., Holley, C.D., Garland, T., Diekhoff, G., and Evans, S.H. (1979) Development and evaluation of a learning strategy training programme *Journal of Educational Psychology* 71(1) 64–73

Davies, J. and Easterby-Smith, M.P.V. (1984) Learning and developing from managerial work experiences *Journal of Management Studies* 21(2) 169–183

Dewey, J. (1916) *Democracy and Education* New York. Macmillan

Dilts, R., Grinder, J., Bandler, R., Bandler, L.C., De Lozier, J. (1980) *Neuro-Linguistic Programming Vol. I* Cupertino, California: Meta Publications

Dolley, J. (1984) *Open University Manpower Services Commission Community Project August 1983–July 1984. Interim Evaluation of a Collaborative Project* IET, The Open University

Duda, R. et al. (1978) *Development of the Prospector Consultation System for Mineral Exploration* Final Report, SRI International, Palo Alto, CA

Ebner, D.G. et al. (1984) Videodiscs can improve instructional efficiency *Instructional Monitor*

Elton, L.R.B., Gillham, B. and Stoane, C. (1984) Editing Open Tech materials. In *Project Development Papers* Open Tech Training and Support Unit

Elton, L.R.B., Hodgson, V., O'Connell, S. (1979) Study counselling at the University of Surrey. In Hills, P.J. (Ed.) *Study Courses and Counselling* Guildford: Society for Research into Higher Education

Eurich, Nell P. (1985) *Corporate Classrooms* Princeton

Evison, R., and Horobin, R. (1985) *How to Change Yourself and Your World* 2nd Edition. Sheffield: Co-Counselling Phoenix

Farnes, N. (Ed.) (1979) *Community Education with the Open University — A Collection of Papers. The Open University Vol. 1, 1974–1979* The Open University

Farnes, N. (1984) *Community Education with the Open University — A Collection of Papers. The Open University Vol. 2, 1979–1984* The Open University

Farnes, N. (1985a) *Community Education Plan for 1986* Community Education, The Open University

Farnes, N. (1985b) *Future Sponsored Places Schemes: a discussion paper. Community Education* The Open University, Internal Community Education Paper Ref. CE3/71/3

Farnes, N., Ballard, A., Jones, M. and Baines, S. (1986) *A Review of a Collaborative Health Education Programme 1976–1986* Community Education, The Open University

Faure, E., Herrern, F., Kaddoura, A-R., Lopes, H., Petrousky, A.V., Rahmerna, M., Ward, F.C. (1972) *Learning to Be* Paris: Unesco

Feigenbaum, E.A., Buchanan, B.G. and Lederberg, J. (1971)·On generality and problem solving: a case study using the DENDRAL program. In B. Meltzer and D. Michie (Eds) *Machine Intelligence, Vol. 6* Edinburgh: Edinburgh University Press

Fordham, P., Poulton, G. and Randle, L. (1979) *Learning Networks in Adult Education: Non-Formal Education on a Housing Estate* London: Routledge and Kegan Paul

Freire, P. (1972) *Cultural Action for Freedom* Penguin Books

Gibbs, G. (1981) *Teaching Students to Learn. A Student-Centred Approach* Milton Keynes: Open University Press

Gibbs, G., Morgan, A. and Taylor, E. (1980) *A Review of the Research of Ference Marton and the Goteburg Group* Study Methods Group Report No. 2, The Open University

Glatter, R. and Wedell, E.G. (1971) *Study By Correspondence* London: Longmans

Grafton-Small, R. and Linstead, S. (1985) Portcullis and Clevely: a necessary edge? *Management Education and Development* 16 (1) 41–47

Hampden-Turner, C. (1971) *Radical Man* London: Duckworth

Harrington, F.A. (1977) *The Future of Adult Education* San Fransisco: Jossey-Bass

Hayes-Roth, F., Waterman, D.A. and Lenat, D.B. (1983) *Building Expert Systems* Reading, Mass.: Addison-Wesley

Hills, P.J. (1979) Communication between student and teacher, In Hills, P.J. (Ed.) *Study Courses and Counselling* Guildford: Society for Research into Higher Education

Holmberg, Borje (1985) *Status and Trends of Distance Education* 2nd revised edition, Lund/Sweden

Honey, P. and Mumford, A. (1982) *Manual of Learning Styles* London: P. Honey

Honey, P. and Mumford, A. (1983) *Using Your Learning Styles* London: P. Honey

Howard, N. (1971) *Paradoxes of Rationality, Theory of Meta Games and Political Behaviour* Cambridge, Mass.: MIT Press

Hudson, K. (1985) The four essentials of training *Training and Development* Journal of the Institute of Training and Development

Hume, D. (1963) *An Enquiry Concerning Human Understanding* New York: Washington Square Press

Hurley, S. and Gearing, B. (1983) Alternative use for Social Workers *Teaching at a Distance* 24, 55–61

Illich, I.D. (1973) *Deschooling Society* Harmondsworth: Penguin

James, K. (1980) The development of senior managers for the future. In Beck, J. and Cox, C. *Advances in Management Education* Chichester: J. Wiley

Juch, A.H. (1983) *Personal Development* Chichester: J. Wiley

Kelly, G.A. (1970) A brief introduction to personal construct theory In Bannister, D. (Ed.) *Perspective in Construct Theory* Academic Press

Kenyon, K.M. (1964) *Beginning in Archaeology* London: Dent & Sons

Kettner, W.D. and Carr, E.P. (1983) *A training effectiveness analysis of standard techniques and the videodisc microprocessor system in the field radio repairer course* VS Army Signal Centre, Fort Gordon, Georgia

Kiesler, C.A. (1971) *The Psychology of Commitment* New York: Academic Press

Kirkup, G. (1985) *The Use and Potential of CEEFAX in the Open University* Information Technology Programme Technical Report No. 5. The Open University

Koestler, A. (1975) *The Act of Creation* London: Picador

Kolb, D.A., Rubin, I.M. and McIntyre, J.M. (1974) *Organizational Psychology: An Experiential Approach* Englewood Cliffs, New Jersey: Prentice Hall

Lakoff, G. and Johnson, M. (1980) *Metaphors we Live by* Chicago: University Press

Lambers, K. and Griffiths, M. (1983) Adapting materials for informal learning groups *Teaching at a Distance* 23, 30–39

Lampikowski, Kari, Mantere, Pertti (1975) *The Guidance System in Distance Education* Helsinki

Laurillard, D. (1979) The processes of student learning *Higher Education* 8, 395–410

Lilley, A. and Calder, J. (1978) *Community Education Courses: Student Demographics Analysis 2. Summary* CEEG Project Memo No.6, The Open University

Lilley, A. (1980) *The Local Radio Experiment* CEEG Paper No.19, The Open University

Lindsey, J. (1984) The challenge of designing for interactive video *Instructional Innovator*

Macquarrie, J. (1973) *Existentialism* Harmondsworth: Penguin Books

McDermott, J. (1984) R1 revisited: four years in the trenches *AI Magazine* 5 (3) 21–32

McDonald, R. (1984) *Recommendations for Staff Development: MBA and FMDP Distance Learning Programmes* University of Strathclyde Business School internal report, August 1984

Marsh, J. (1983) The boredom of study: a study of boredom *Management Education and Development* 14 (2) 120–135

Marton, F. (1983) Beyond individual differences *Educational Psychology* 3, 289–303

Marton, F. and Säljö, R. (1976) On qualitative differences in learning: outcome and process *British Journal of Educational Psychology* 46, 4–11

Maslow, A.H. (1943) A theory of human motivations *Psychological Review* 50, 370–396

Mathieson, D.F. (1971) *Correspondence Study: a summary review of the research and development literature* New York National Home Study Council/E.R.I.C. Clearinghouse on Adult Education

Mead, M. (1976) *Culture and Commitment* (revised edition) New York: Columbia University Press

Merton, R.K. and Kendal, P.L. (1946) The focussed interview *American Journal of Sociology* 5, 541–557

Mitchell, F.D. (1979) A micro-analytical procedure to improve instructional materials. In Page, G.T., and Whitlock, Q.A. (Eds) *Aspects of Educational Technology, Vol. XIII: Educational Technology Twenty Years On* London: Kogan Page, pp. 349–354

Moralee, S. (1986) Expert systems — some user experience. In O'Shea, T., Self, J. and Thomas, G. (Eds) *Intelligent Knowledge Based Systems: an Introduction* London: Harper & Row

Mumford, A. (1985) *Effectiveness in Learning: Learning to Learn.* Buckingham: IMCB

Naisbitt, J. (1982) *Megatrends* New York: Warner Books

NCC Ltd (1985) *Interactive Video — design and development* National Computer Centre

Nix, Joseph H. (1985) Coast guard training for course development *NHSC News* Washington

Northcott, P. (1985) University of Strathclyde Business School internal AIP memo dated 25 July 1985

O'Hanlon, W. and Wilk, J. (1987) *Shifting Contexts* New York: Guildford Press

Olsen, L. and Fazio, R.D. (1983) Journal 'The Shoemaker's Children' *Training and Development*

O'Shea, T. Self, J. and Thomas, G. (Eds) *Intelligent Knowledge Based Systems: an Introduction* London: Harper & Row

The Open University (1969) *Charter* Paragraph 3. The Open University

The Open University (1980) *Health Choices* Community Education, The Open University

The Open University (1984) *Continuing Education Guide 1985–1986* Academic Administration, The Open University

The Open University (1985) *Community Education Courses and Packs* Community Education, The Open University

Pedler, M. (1986) Developing within the organisation: experiences of management self development groups *Management Education and Development* 17 (1) 5–21

Percy, K.A. and Ramsden, P. (1980) *Independent Study: Two Examples from English Higher Education* Guildford: Society for Research Into Higher Education

Perraton, H. (1981) A theory for distance education *Prospects* 11 (1)

Perry, W.G. (1970) *Forms of Intellectual and Ethical Development in the College Years: a Scheme* New York: Holt Rinehart and Winston

Peters, Otto (1971) Theoretical aspects of correspondence instruction In McKenzie, O. and Christensen, E.L. *The Changing World of Correspondence Study International* Readings, Penn.: Pennsylvania State University Press.

Peters, O. (1981) Distance teaching and industrial production: a comparative interpretation in outline (translation of pernstudium und industrielle produktion: skizze einer vergleichenden interpretation) In R. Hansehmann (1981) *Okonomische theorie und wirtschaftlicher praxis — festschrift zum 65* Herne/Berlin: Verlag Neue Wirtschafts-Briefe

Pirsig, R.M. (1974) *Zen and the Art of Motor Cycle Maintenance* London: Bodley Head

Ramsden, P., Entwistle, N.J. (1981) Effects of academic departments on students' approaches to studying *British Journal of Educational Psychology* 51, 368–383

Ramsden, P. (1983) Institutional variations in British students' approaches to learning and experiences of teaching *Higher Education* 12, 691–705

Revans, R.W. (1979) The nature of action learning *Management Education and Development* 10 (1) 3–23

Revans, R.W. (1984) On the learning equation in 1984 *Management Education and Development* 15 (3) 209–220

Rhodes, D.M., and Azbell, J.W. (1985) Designing interactive video professionally *Training and Development Journal* 39 (12) 31–33

Roberts, D. (1984) Ways and means of reducing early student drop-out rates *Distance Education* 5 (1) 50–71

Robinson, B. (1981) Support for Student Learning. Chapter 8 in Kaye, A & Rumble, G. (Eds) *Distance Teaching for Higher and Adult Education* London: Croom Helm/Open University Press

Rogers, C. (1983) *Freedom to Learn. For the '80s* Colombus Ohio: Charles, E. Merrill Publishing Co., Bell and Hewell, 2nd edition

Rosenthal, R. and Jacobsen, L. (1968) *Pygmalion in the Classroom* New York: Holt, Rinehart & Winston

Rossi, E.L. (Ed.) (1980) *Collected Papers of Milton H. Erikson* (four volumes) New York: Irvington

Rudd, E. (1975) *The Highest Education: A Study of Graduate Education in Britain* London: Routledge and Kegan Paul

Rumble, G. (1982) *The Open University of the United Kingdom* Milton Keynes: OU (DERG)

Salancik, G.T. (1977) Commitment and the control of organisational behaviour and belief In Staw, B. and Salancik, G.R. (Eds) *New Directions in Organisational Behaviour* Chicago: St Clair Press

Säljö, R. (1979) Learning in the learner's perspective: II: differences in awareness *Reports from the Institute of Education* 77, University of Gothenburg

Sandewaal, E. (1978) Programming in the interactive environment: the LISP experience *Computing Surveys*, 10, 35–71

Sarason, I.A. (1975) Test anxiety, attention and the general problem of anxiety. In Spielberger, C.D. and Sarason, I.A., *Stress and Anxiety* New York: Halstead Press

Schmeck, R.R., Grove, E. (1979) Academic achievement and individual differences in learning processes *Applied Psychological Measurement* 3, 43–49

Schon, D. (1971) *Beyond the Stable State* New York: W.W. Norton

Schwalbe, Heinz (1972) The integration of face-to-face and distance education *Epistolodidaktika* London

Schwalbe, Heinz (1973) Aspects of students' motivation *Epistolodidaktika* London

Schwalbe, Heinz (1977a) What cost effectiveness in distance education means *Epistolodidaktika* London

Schwalbe, Heinz (1977b) Tutors' training or training of distance educators *Epistolodidaktika* London

Shortliffe, E. (1976) *Computer Based Medical Consultations: MYCIN* New York: American Elsevier

Skemp, R.R. (1971) *The Psychology of Learning Mathematics* Harmondsworth: Penguin Books

Smith, K.C., (1979) *External Studies at New England: a silver jubilee review* Armidale: University of New England Press, Australia

Special report on premiums and incentives (1984) *Campaign* September

Stainton-Rogers, W. (1983) Alternative uses of materials *Teaching at a Distance* 24, 49–54

Stewart, D. et al. (Eds) *Distance Education: International Perspectives* London: Croom Helm

Stuart, R. (1984) Maximising managers' day-to-day learning. In Cox, C. and Beck, J. (Eds) *Management Development: Advances in Theory and Practice* Wiley

Stuart, R., and Holmes, L. (1982) Successful trainer styles *Journal of European Industrial Training* 6 (4) 17–23

Svensson, L. (1977) On qualitative differences in learning: III — study skill and learning *British Journal of Educational Psychology* 47, 233–243

Swift, B. (1981) Public awareness of the Open University *Teaching at a Distance* 19, 79–84

Taylor, E. (1984) *Orientation to Study: a Longitudinal Investigation of Two Degrees in One University* Unpublished PhD dissertation, University of Surrey

Taylor, E., Morgan, A. and Gibbs, G. (1981) The "orientation" of Open University Foundation students to their studies *Teaching at a Distance* 20 (Winter)

Taylor, E., Morgan, A. and Gibbs, G. (1983) Student perceptions of gains from studying D101 *Institutional Research Review* 2, 133–147

Thomas, L.F., Harri-Augstein, E.S. (1977) Learning to learn: the personal construction and exchange of meaning. In Howe, M.J. (Ed.) *Adult Learning. Psychological Research and Applications* John Wiley & Sons

Thomas, P.R., Bain, J.D. (1982) Consistency in learning strategies *Higher Education* 11, 249–259

Thompson, E.P. (1965) *The Making of the English Working Class* London: Victor Gollancz

Toffler, A. (1974) *Learning For Tomorrow* New York: Random House

Toffler, A. (1980) *The Third Wave* New York: Bantom Books

Vallee, J. (1984) *The Network Revolution: Confessions of a Computer Scientist* Harmondsworth: Penguin Books

Van Leer Project Team (1981) *The Development and Use of Parent Educational Materials* The Open University

Venables Report (1976) *Report of the Committee on Continuing Education* The Open University, p. 14, para.1

Vroom, V.H. (1964) *Work and Motivation* Wiley

Watzlawick, P. (1978) *The Language of Change* New York: Basic Books

Watzlawick, P. (Ed.) (1984) *The Invented Reality* New York: Norton

Watzlawick, P., Weakland, J.M. and Fisch, R. (1974) *Change: Principles of Problem Formation and Problem Resolution* New York: Norton

Welsh, T. (1981) *An Economic Exploration of Aspects of Organisational Performance* Continuing Education, The Open University

Welsh, T. (1982) *The Measurement of Programme Promotion Performance of Continuing Education. The Open University* CEREG Paper No.5, The Open University

Welsh, T. (1983) *Continuing Education. Open University as 'Self-Financing' 'Commercially' Viable* CEREG Discussion Document No. 1, The Open University

Wheaton, J.A. (1984) We hear what we see: the marriage of audio and video *Videodisc and Optical Disk*

Wheeler, Sir. M. (1956) *Archaeology From The Earth.* Harmondsworth: Penguin.

Williams, W., Calder, J. and Moore, M. (1981) Local support services in continuing education *Teaching at a Distance* 19, 40–58

Williamson, J. (1978) *Decoding Advertisements* Marion Boyars

Wilson, C. (1980) *The New Existentialism* London: Wildwood House (previously published as *Introduction to the New Existentialism* Hutchinson 1966)

Woodley, A. (1981) *The Open University of the United Kingdom* Paris: European Cultural Foundation, Institute of Education

Woodley, et al. (1983) *Mature Students* Final Report to the Department of Education and Science of the Research Project on Mature Student Participation in Education

Woodley, F., Ballard, A. and Sayer, B. (1984a) *Support Models for Community Education Summary Report Part 1: Regional Offices and Local Co-ordinators* CEREG Paper No.17, The Open University

Woodley, F., Ballard, A. and Sayer, B. (1984b) *Support Models for Community Education. Summary Report Part 2: Collaborative Projects* CEREG Paper No.29, The Open University

Woolley, Sir. L. (1937) *Digging Up the Past* Harmondsworth: Penguin

Wright, J. (1982) *Learning to Learn in Higher Education* London: Croom Helm

Young, M., Perraton, H., Jenkings, J. and Doggs, T. (1980) *Distance Teaching for the Third World* London: Routledge

Zander, Ernst (1984) Organizational and personnel-related aspects of leadership in large companies *Improving Production and Productivity* Bochum

The Society for Research into Higher Education

The Society exists both to encourage and co-ordinate research and development into all aspects of Higher Education, including academic, organizational and policy issues; and also to provide a forum for debate, verbal and printed. Through its activities, it draws attention to the significance of research into, and development in, Higher Education and to the needs of scholars in this field. (It is not concerned with research generally, except, for instance, as a subject of study.)

The Society's income derives from subscriptions, book sales, conferences and specific grants. It is wholly independent. Its corporate members are institutions of higher education, research institutions and professional, industrial, and governmental bodies. Its individual members include teachers and researchers, administrators and students. Members are found in all parts of the world and the Society regards its international work as amongst its most important activities.

The Society discusses and comments on policy, organizes conferences and encourages research. Under the Imprint SRHE & OPEN UNIVERSITY PRESS, it is a specialist publisher, having some 40 titles in print. It also publishes *Studies in Higher Education* (three times a year) which is mainly concerned with academic issues, *Higher Education Quarterly* (formerly *Universities Quarterly*) which will be mainly concerned with policy issues, *Research into Higher Education Abstracts* (three times a year), and a *Bulletin* (six times a year).

The Society's committees, study groups and branches are run by members (with help from a small staff at Guildford), and aim to provide a form for discussion. The groups at present include a Teacher Education Study Group, a Staff Development Group, a Women in Higher Education Group and a Continuing Education Group which may have had their own organization, subscriptions or publications; (eg the *Staff Development Newsletter*). The Governing Council, elected by members, comments on current issues; and discusses policies with leading figures, notably at its evening Forums. The Society organizes seminars on current research for officials of DES and other ministries, an Anglo-American series on standards, and is in touch with bodies in the UK such as the NAB, CVCP, UGC, CNAA and the British Council, and with sister-bodies overseas. Its current research projects include one on the relationship between entry qualifications and degree results, directed by Prof. W.D. Furneaux (Brunel) and one on questions of quality directed by Prof. G.C. Moodie (York). A project on the evaluation of the research standing of university departments is in preparation. The Society's conferences are often held jointly. Annual Conferences have considered 'Professional Education' (1984), 'Continuing Education' (1985, with Goldsmiths' College) 'Standards and Criteria in Higher Education' (1986, with Bulmershe CHE), 'Restructuring' (1987, with the City of Birmingham Polytechnic) and 'Academic Freedom' (1988, the University of Surrey). Other conferences have considered the DES 'Green Paper' (1985, with the Times Higher Education

Supplement), and 'The First-Year Experience' (1986, with the University of South Carolina and Newcastle Polytechnic). For some of the Society's conferences, special studies are commissioned in advance, as 'Precedings'.

Members receive free of charge the Society's *Abstracts,* annual conference Proceedings (or 'Precedings'), *Bulletin and International Newsletter* and may buy SRHE & OPEN UNIVERSITY PRESS books at booksellers' discount. Corporate members also receive the Society's journal *Studies in Higher Education* free (individuals at a heavy discount). They may also obtain *Evaluation Newsletter* and certain other journals at a discount, including the NFER *Register of Educational Research.* There is a substantial discount to members, and to staff of corporate members, on annual and some other conference fees.